SAY THE UNSAID
THROUGH
ANALYTICS

EXTENDING FRONTIERS OF ANALYTICS

MALAYA ROUT,
HARIHARAN RAJARAM,
JYOTHSNA SRAVANTHI

INDIA · SINGAPORE · MALAYSIA

Notion Press

Old No. 38, New No. 6
McNichols Road, Chetpet
Chennai - 600 031

First Published by Notion Press 2019
Copyright © Malaya Rout, Hariharan Rajaram, Jyothsna Sravanthi 2019
All Rights Reserved.

ISBN 978-1-64546-865-3

Contents

List of Images

List of Tables

Foreword

The authors of this book are competent and seasoned data scientists who have cross-functional experience of various industries and data science concepts. I am happy to write this foreword for this completely anarchic book on data science. I know these authors as my colleagues working with Verizon India, responsible for churning large data sets to bring as much knowledge as possible using various data science tools and techniques. We have discussed, debated, brainstormed and challenged various nuances of data science concepts every other day. We have also shared our practical analytics challenges among ourselves and sought valuable inputs which have helped us in successfully delivering very complex projects. I am into data science field for the past 20 years. I haven't read a compilation of data science unorthodox thoughts like this. I have worked in various data science product based companies, applied and led several data science projects in service industries and captive companies. I have played various roles in analytics such as teacher, trainer, consultant, senior operations manager, practice lead, SME, Senior Architect and Senior Program manager.

The topics in this book are hard-learned thoughts of these authors who have spent a good amount of time in the field of data science. I am reminded of a discussion with these authors some time ago on various analytics jargons such as *analytics, data science, data mining, machine learning, deep learning* et cetera. If you browse through the internet for answers, you will be flooded with numerous school of thoughts which will definitely confuse you. But now I can see that these authors have spent good time in collating the meaningful and practical differences among these buzz words through this book. I am sure these explanations are brought to this book after discussing with eminent data scientists in the market, after discussing thoroughly in various forums and after lots of deliberations.

This book keeps in mind different communities of readers. For the readers who are aspiring to become data scientists, the book covers topics such as *Putting jargon-olytics in perspective, Analytics: where do we use, Survival analysis, Data based opinion versus opinion based opinion et cetera.* For budding data scientists the book has topics such as *What makes a good data scientist, Don't build a model – build a solution, Summarize basic modeling techniques, train and test datasets, What should the data science practitioner be careful about, The underplayed EDA* et cetera. This book also covers few different perspectives on data science which could amuse data science practitioners as well such as *Hop a little jump a little from stage to stage, Text analytics in its deceivingly innocent form, What is so deep about deep learning, Machining machine learning, When can data science fail, Predict using clustering* et cetera. This book also enlightens us through practical examples for better comprehension of data science concepts such as *Defect prediction modeling for better test management using MLR, the role of analytics in psychiatric disorders, A customized ensemble model* et cetera.

Overall, this book will walk alongside you through your data science career and be a good companion whenever you need one. Happy reading!

By Sudeesh Sankaravel, Data Scientist and Senior Program Manager, Verizon India

We would love to hear from you - might be on this book or just about anything outside the realm of this book that four friends could talk about. If you have an unconventional idea on data science that's killing you to come out in the open, write to us. If you debated with your mentor today on a topic but could not arrive at an agreement, write to us. If you became a 'thoughtful you' for a considerable duration today, write to us. Our email is **datasizen@gmail.com**

Acknowledgement

At the outset, we thank our families for unconditionally supporting us in all our ventures. This is not a book created solely by the three of us. Many individuals played a pivotal role in bringing this book to reality.

We thank all those who reviewed the book and offered their remarks. Names are listed in alphabetical order – Akihiro Sato, Dr. Ananta Charan Ojha, Neelakanta Matadam, Partha Vijayan, Radhakrishnan Guhan, Rajesh Kumar, Sriram Lamsal, Vrushali Sarfare and Yogananth M.

We sincerely thank Sudeesh Sankaravel for writing the foreword and being a sounding board to all our unconventional thoughts in the context of this book and outside of it too.

We also thank our workplace for giving us the opportunity to shape our skills and talent.

We are hugely indebted to our friends and readers who engaged with us on a variety of topics and use cases in Data Science. They read and re-read our content to ensure that it is meaningful to a host of readers. This helped us draw out the unsaid and kindled us continuously to do more.

1. Putting Jargon-Olytics in Perspective

(Each jargon has a story underneath)

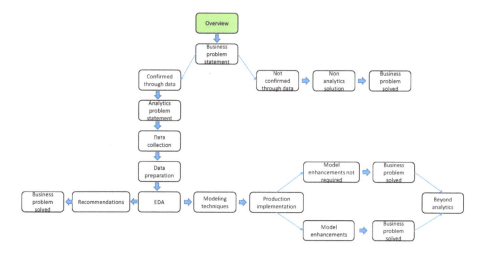

A flowchart is provided in each article which depicts the flow of an analytics project through various stages. The box highlighted in green tells us where the focus of the current article lies.

Needless to say that analytics jargons confuse us. Many a time we end up using them quite loosely. Following is a list the knowledge of which I acquired from my mentor (mentioning this is important because in case of disagreement between you and me, I will straightaway blame my mentor!).

Artificial Intelligence: Is the overarching field existing as a counterpart to human intelligence. It could be non-data based or data based. Examples of non-data based AI are robotics, instruction led machines, et cetera. Data based AI is called Data Science. Then we have Artificial Specific Intelligence and Artificial Generic Intelligence. Let me pretend here that I know both and suggest that you google them. Enough of laziness!

Data Science: Is purely data based. It encapsulates all activities of a typical Data Science project such as data collection, data preparation, exploratory data analysis, modeling, presentation, et cetera.

Machine Learning: Is the ability to make a computer carry out specific tasks without the need for explicit programming. It learns the task based on patterns and behavior of data. Then it recommends decisions using data similar to which it has learned from.

Deep Learning: Is an extension of Machine Learning. It includes neural networks which are multi-layered learning structures.

Cognitive Learning: A bit uncertain about how to put this one. Appears to me as when we sense collective inputs from various sources and identify what the event is.

Reinforcement Learning: It is a class of Machine Learning which does not really depend on patterns of data but rather works on Trial and Error method wherein the process (agents) would continuously expect for feedback/response for its action and determine whether to continue or make a new trial eventually making sure all its actions are right.

Business Intelligence: Mostly reporting. It includes the descriptive and diagnostic levels of analytics. It deals with explicit information.

Data Mining: It is the process of extracting known and hidden patterns from large data sets by using techniques involving Machine Learning coupled with statistical methods. It deals with implicit information.

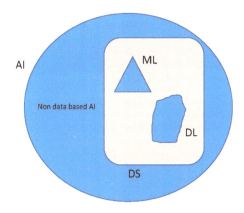

The Landscape

Analytics: Happy to say that we can use DS and analytics interchangeably. Wait! Don't get too carried away. Analytics is basically art plus science. Now that the field is becoming very scientific and standardized, let's use DS.

2. Analytics or Not. Checklist

(A meeting without an agenda is like eating without food)

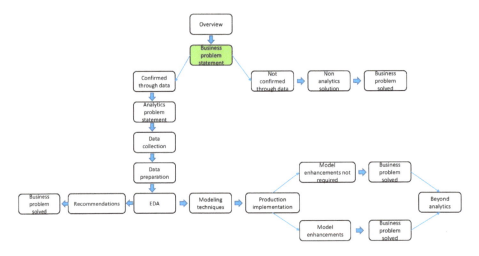

Once I asked a group of budding data scientists. Can all business problems be solved using analytics? The silence was the closest response.

I am tempted to think of a checklist as a set of entry criteria which will help us decide whether analytics is the right choice for a problem.

Historical Data

Data science is the data part of Artificial Intelligence. It works solely on the presence of relevant historical data. Historical data here refers to recorded data taken in the past based on which patterns can be inferred. Future decisions can be made when similar data patterns appear. Do we have enough data? By the way how much is enough?

Consistent Story

Does data confirm the business problem statement? If not, work with stakeholders to understand why there is no reflection of the problem in data.

Sub Business Problems

Can we break the parent business problem into multiple sub business problems?

Analytics Problem Statement

We should be able to transform each sub business problem into multiple possible analytics problem statements.

Why

Understanding the reason behind the problem. Can EDA alone solve the problem? Right and quick?

Concurrence with Stakeholders

Not necessarily every possible analytics solution should be picked up at one go. Discuss with business representatives and choose one out of three (just saying) solutions to start with.

Expertise

Do we have statistical, exploratory, machine learning, visualization, domain and programming expertise?

Software and Hardware

Availability of software and hardware in line with the volume of data is essential (obviously).

Function

We should know which department of the organization is going to use our solution.

Consumption

Is there a destination where the solution will be consumed by users? It requires development activity.

Analytics Level

What level of analytics exercise is suitable to solve the problem – descriptive, diagnostic, predictive or prescriptive?

Who Will Pay?

Do we have a sponsorship from the requestor?

Cost-Benefit Analysis

Is long term estimated benefit greater than the cost of doing analytics? Do we know how to tag growth which was caused by analytics?

Adoption

Adoption measurement and adoption strategy are key. What's our estimate of adoption? How do we plan to increase adoption? A brilliant solution not adopted by anyone is not a solution at all.

This list might not be complete as yet. Feel free to suggest. However, it could be a nice starting point for us to think.

3. Data Based Opinion versus Opinion Based Opinion

(Opinion based opinion is like weather. It always changes)

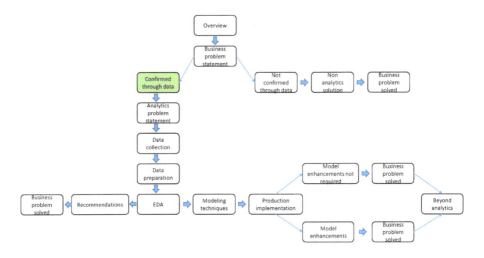

Data is the closest one can get to reality through. Why don't I claim that data gives us the complete truth? This is because it's very challenging to capture soft attributes such as emotion, sentiment, mood, stress level, et cetera. in the form of data.

Hard attributes such as age, salary, temperature, family size, et cetera. are easy to capture and interpret. However, soft attributes go a long way to impact our decision-making process. This is why I don't believe that data is a complete reality.

Data shows us the direction in our journey. It leads us to understand the past and get prepared for the future. Usually, we study the behavior of a subject in the past, determine the relationship among the playing variables, extrapolate and predict how the subject is going to behave in the future whenever a similar situation is encountered.

Exploration of data unveils insights enabling businesses to grow and customers to have a smooth personalized experience. For example, the scientific treatment of data helps in early detection and timely action on critical diseases.

Opinion formed from analysis of data is reliable more often than not. I know. I have already pointed out the lack of completeness in any data set. I am aware of the difficulties with missing soft attributes. On the other hand, an opinion formed from other's opinion without strong backing is harmful. Such an opinion might turn out to be nothing more than gossip!!

Data is the new gold. Data not analyzed and sitting idle in data stores is a huge opportunity missed. Let's stop writing now and let's go and explore some data!

4. Analytics. Where Do We Use?

(Use things the right way even if the outcome seems unfavorable)

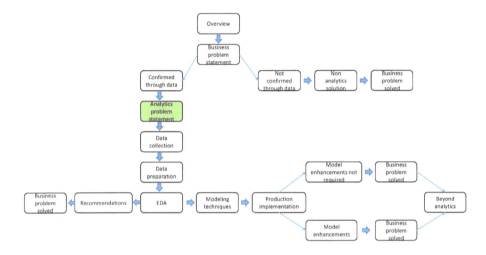

Who are the consumers of analytics output? Business organizations. They are the ones who capture and store data. They wish to mine the intelligence from data and use it for improving the way they do business. No one wants to miss the bus that goes to a competitive advantage. Hence the buzz.

Analytics for B2B is different from that in B2C. I would say more challenging. B2B has a lesser volume of data, longer duration of deal cycles, lower churn, and different business problems and relies a lot on relationships built over many years. You may often hear a business user remarking that they know more about their business than what a model could recommend.

Having said that let me list out a few out of a plethora of analytics applications. There could be another hundred, but I will stop much earlier than that. It's up to you to take the idea and find the rest.

1. Prospect segmentation

2. Sales prediction

3. Loan accept/reject recommendation

4. Loan amount recommendation

5. Revenue forecasting

6. Cross-selling

7. Credit card fraud detection

8. Estimation of service ticket resolution time

9. Customer comments sentiment analysis

10. Spam email/SMS identification

11. Likelihood of a quotation converting to order

12. Suggest problem category from its description

13. Analyze intervals between various checkpoints in a business process and identify the scope of improvement

14. Identify which products should be placed together in a retail store

15. Predict machine failure

16. Predict which disease a patient will suffer from next month

17. Will a person suffer from kidney failure next year?

18. Personalization of features and recommendations for my profile with an online retail store

19. Churn

20. Predicting sports match outcomes

21. Weather forecasting

I know this list is not nearly exhaustive. Don't worry. I hope you get the idea. Now come up with more.

5. What Makes a Good Data Scientist?

(Talent does not make one successful. Attitude does)

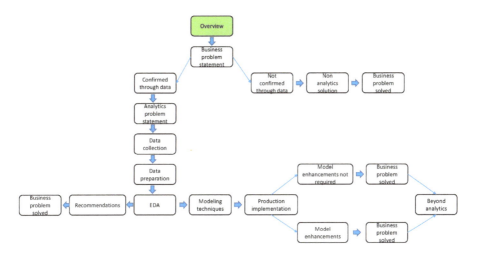

I don't promise to answer all your questions. But I promise to give you enough food for thought.

If you call someone a data scientist then he should be a good data explorer, good machine learning expert and a good visualization/presentation expert covering the three broad phases of an analytics exercise. In addition, he should have a good understanding of the domain or industry he is solving the problem for. I usually divide the field horizontally into two slices – applications and concepts. Again broadly. Place a couple of more slices if you wish. This makes me believe that there would be a group of skillets available focusing only on applying a technique, using a method, looking at the diagnostics and concluding. The emergence of drag and drop tools for exploratory data analysis, model building and the pursuit of automatic semi-insight generation will require data scientists to be good only in applying a method. That scares me a bit.

I would imagine that someone who understands from the ground up the statistics, the logic behind every parameter and the reasoning of every decision taken is in the right direction. Analytics programming languages such as R, Python and SAS, unlike automated tools, give you excellent flexibility and opportunity to play with concepts if you ask the right questions.

Data science is as much an art as it is a science. There is only a limited prescription of how to ideally carry out a data science project. Success mostly depends on the right choice of influencing variables, selection of data exploration techniques, choice of modeling techniques, parameter tuning and the choice of thresholds for each diagnostic metric. If two out of seven model diagnostics fail should you reject the model? I can't answer that for you! Find out. Hint. Rank order the diagnostics based on the problem statement.

The data scientist should also be a good programmer. Don't forget that he needs excellent soft skills to convey technical ideas and outputs in a simple language for stakeholders. Are we asking too much from our data scientist!

If I can answer in two lines, I would say a data scientist first should be a good human being which is reflected in the choice of problem statements he solves. Is he detecting cancer in a person early or is he predicting whether the stock market will go up or down tomorrow! My apologies in advance to the group of data scientists it hurts. Just my thought.

6. Don't Build a Model, Build a Solution

(Build relationships, not houses)

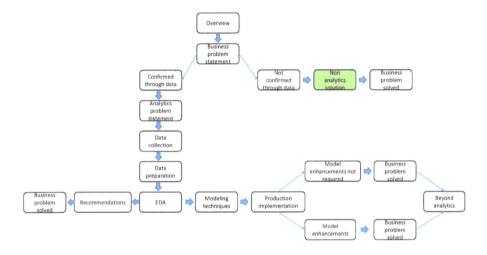

Technical prowess is essential to be a good data scientist. Business and functional knowledge are crucial too. Technical skills would encapsulate expertise in statistical concepts, programming, visualization and presentation.

A model that does not solve a business problem well but is used frequently to comply with the pressure of adopting analytics is like cancer to business. On the other hand, a model which recommends well but is not used enough by users due to lack of sensitization of benefits of analytics is a loss of opportunity. Either way, data is not playing the pivotal role it should play in giving a competitive advantage to the organization.

Data science is not machine learning (training the model) alone. It includes all activities from understanding the business problem to finally implementing and monitoring the solution in the live environment. The outcome of this exercise should be an end to end solution that could flourish either standalone or in tandem with an existing IT application. Most of the cases I have seen belong to the second category. Might be I have not seen enough yet.

Attributing a revenue growth to an analytics solution alone is very tricky. One has to be careful to eliminate all other possible boosters of revenue in that case. Conversion of a business problem statement to an analytics problem statement is equally tricky. For example, let's say that the business problem is that the revenue of the organization is going down consistently over the last four years. Decide on the scope (products, timeline, extent) of the problem yourself. It doesn't matter in this context. What could be the various possible analytics problem statements? 1) Identify high potential products that the sales team can focus on 2) Identify the high potential prospects that the marketing team could target with their customized and personalized campaigns 3) Market mix. How much to spend on which channel for best returns 4) Forecast next quarter sales and alert if necessary with recommendations 5) Predict ticket resolution time and improve customer experience.

The above options need to be discussed with business stakeholders. One or more of them should be selected to build a solution on. Each option above has a unique way of increasing revenue. I think what if we can quantify the impact of each of the five solutions on revenue and then pick up the top two or three solutions. Just keep in mind that all five solutions need not cater to the same business team, which means that five different teams can come forward simultaneously and show an interest. Ranking will help to prioritize.

Training a model is not a mandatory activity in a data science project. You would often encounter situations where an exploratory data analysis (EDA) by itself was able to provide you the necessary insights. When the business team uses the insight to solve their problem, it becomes an elegant analytics solution.

7. Predicting the Past

(What does your past have in store for you?)

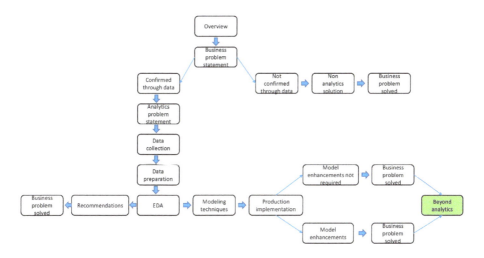

We usually talk about predicting what's going to happen in the future. How do we put predicting the past in context now? An oxymoron, isn't it? I would say descriptive and diagnostic analytics, the first two levels of analytics, occupy this space. Descriptive data science gives us the ability to understand WHAT has happened in the past through various visualization techniques. Techniques could be simple scatter plots, histograms or bar graphs – doesn't matter. Diagnostic data science, on the other hand, revolves around WHY something has happened after identifying what has happened. I usually cite the following example in my talks for data science enthusiasts. Someone studying the trend of sales year over year for a retail chain identifies that there is an evident spike in sales in December each year. If he sends this report along with his observation of the spike to the analytics consumer, then he is carrying out descriptive analytics. He leaves it to the client to interpret the anomaly or distinguishing pattern. However, before sending the report if the data scientist puts in an additional effort to analyze what could be the reasons of the spike then he is performing the next level of analytics which is diagnostic in nature. Reasons could be the holiday season, Christmas, low temperature, snowfall, anything for that matter.

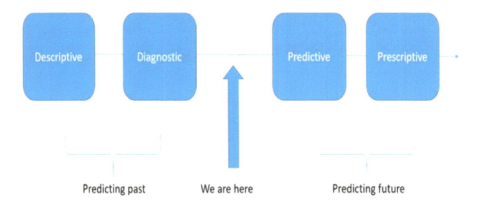

Analytics Levels

8. Predicting Better Than History

(Let's challenge history)

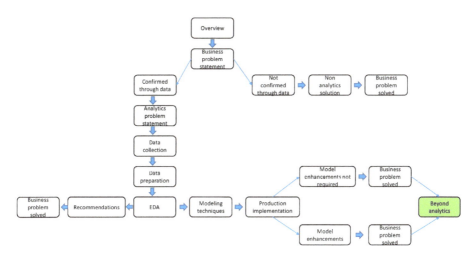

Accept or reject? Go or no go? Buy or build? Outsource or keep in-house? Many a time we find ourselves at these decision points. What if, as a data scientist, I build a statistical model to help me take these decisions? The question that arises next is how much I should rely on the model's recommendation versus my intuition to arrive at a decision. A lot depends on the technical accuracy of the model. 'Technical' because in real life there is no way to ascertain the correctness of the model unless the outcome of our decision is known. This way we calculate the model's real-life usefulness and enhance it if it falls short of expectations.

Imagine we are at a stage when we have to take a call on the extent of belief on the model which is way before we come to know about its real-life accuracy. Comparison of technical diagnostics of the train set and test set is the answer. I am thinking of a scenario when, say, both the train and test accuracies are in the range of 80 percentages which is good.

However, what if the majority of the non-model-based decisions taken in the past two years were incorrect and we have used that historical data as the basis for training the model. The model will try to mimic history and will accurately recommend inaccurate decisions.

How do we work around this? Let me take the example of a loan accept/reject problem statement. Can I introduce a new variable called 'extent of rightness of decision' which could be a value between 0 to 10 in the historical data? I am not saying it is going to be easy! Agree on a threshold value of that variable (for example 7) above which the original Y variable is retained else it is flipped. This forms our derived Y variable which will be used to build the model.

Snapshot of Sample Data

age	salary (lakhs/annum)	family size	location	accept/reject	extent of right-ness (scale of 0 to 10)	derived accept/reject (threshold of flip is 5)
25	10	4	Chennai	accept	3	reject
30	20	2	Bhubaneswar	accept	8	accept
33	15	10	Mumbai	reject	1	accept
22	40	5	Bangalore	reject	10	reject

Arriving at an extent of rightness for each loan application in the past two years and then determining the threshold of the flip are better said than done. We can still find out when an accept decision goes right or wrong.

How do you find out whether a reject decision has gone right or wrong? Especially in decision-making problem scenarios the idea of building a model based on historical data to recommend a course of action makes me ask the question of whether we want to perform as good as history or better than that? I know I have asked than answered more questions!

9. Defect Prediction for Better Test Management

(Who said defects were terrible? They provide jobs)

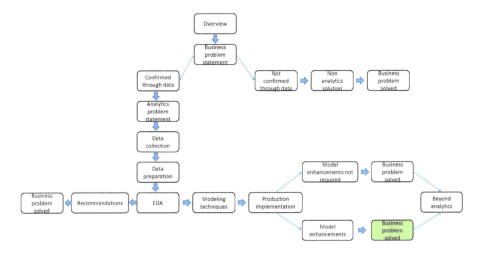

You're heading out on a business trip or a family vacation. One of the first things you do is to check the weather forecast. You would decide whether you need to pack your boots, umbrellas, cotton clothes or thick woolen coats. You would check the temperature trend. You would check with your friends and colleagues about the place you intend to visit. What would have happened if we don't have access to prior information? Would we have packed all the possible protective gear? Would we carry extra cash to buy them at our destination point? Would we plan for the additional discomfort it may result in? It is always good to know beforehand what to expect at the destination.

Handling a project is no different from planning a family vacation. Being able to predict project health is all the more vital today. The Business landscape we are currently operating in is continuously changing. Hordes of new technologies enter into our market with each passing day. You have more uncertainty to deal with. In this context, any information that is available much ahead in our project life cycle helps us better plan and organize. We would like to understand which factors impact the number of system testing defects the most. Here I would be discussing one of the approaches to arrive at a Defect Prediction Model. It can be built using a statistical technique called Multiple Linear Regression (MLR).

We would like to predict the number of system testing defects (y). This becomes our dependent variable. This can be expressed as a Multiple Linear Regression equation: $y = a + bx_1 + cx_2 + \ldots px_{n-1} + qx_n$, where $x_1, x_2 \ldots x_{n-1}, x_n$ are the independent variables. These are the factors that affect our dependent variable. a is the intercept. b, c, … p, q are the corresponding coefficients.

Approach to building this model involves the following steps: data preparation, variable selection, model building and model validation.

We could collect the following information over a large set of projects:

- Number of lines of code
- Number of Unit Testing defects
- Presence of Functional Specifications document
- Presence of Technical Specifications document
- Development Effort
- Size of Development team
- Average Developer experience
- Size of the Test team
- Average Tester experience
- % Delay in the Development schedule
- Programming language used
- Planned System testing Effort
- Number of Test cases
- Number of System testing defects

Data Preparation: As part of this step, treat data collected for any missing values, outliers, single-valued variables, et cetera. Create any derived variables as necessary.

Variable Selection: Select independent variables using Chi-square test of independence and Multicollinearity tests.

Model Building: Divide the data into Train and Test datasets. Build a Multiple Linear Regression model on the Train dataset. Study the model performance metrics.

Model Validation: Validate the model by predicting the number of System testing defects using Test dataset. Compare Train and Test model performance parameters.

From the model, we can identify significant factors that impact the number of system testing defects in a given project. It can be used for defect prediction in future projects. Now that we have a model, we can fine tune our test planning and realize many benefits over time. Listing few of them:

- Having predicted the number of system testing defects managers can optimize Effort estimation, Test scheduling and Resource planning.

- Managers can take note of essential factors impacting the project early in the life cycle and deploy preventive measures. For example, have the right functional and technical specifications documents, do better Unit testing, et cetera.

We should also note that modeling is not a one-off task. The defect prediction modeling is a continuously evolving exercise. Model is as good as the data that is used. Thus, the existing model is fine-tuned continuously with the data available from the new projects. This is how the model becomes robust.

Well, luckily for us when we plan for a trip we have enough sites that provide us information to plan in advance. These are the details ranging from what to pack, where to stay, how much to spend, what to beware of et cetera. Happy traveling!

10. Predicting the Salary of a 120-Year-Old!

(You are never too old to draw a salary)

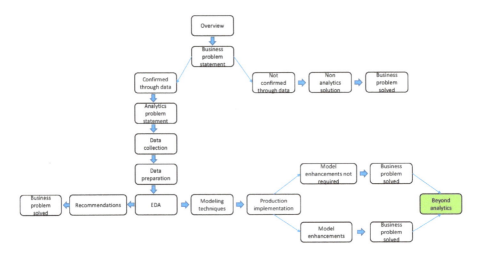

Take this in the context of simple linear regression (SLR). How much does a 5-year-old earn? How much does a 30-year-old or an 80-year-old person earn? Upon plotting a scatter plot, we will loosely conclude that salary increases linearly with age. Why am I saying 'loosely'? Because the relationship might not be linear throughout the range of values of age.

In the most probable case, salary will vary linearly with age between 22 and 62 years of age. Outside this range, it is either 0 or a constant amount (for kids and retired persons respectively).

In this scenario we expect the model to predict correctly when the age is in mid-range. I cannot extrapolate. A question arises. Should I then consider 120 years as an outlier and remove it completely from the dataset? Yes. Might be for now. What if in future due to medical advancements, ages higher than 100 becomes more frequent? I can no longer ignore them. I should accommodate those data points in my train and test sets.

How do we solve this? Few ideas follow. 1) Scope out any age outside the boundaries and declare that the salary could not be predicted in those cases 2) Build a nonlinear model for each of the legs outside the linear range.

If you have noticed you have used your domain knowledge of job and income inadvertently to believe what I said about salary being roughly linear between 22 and 62 years of age.

I want to touch upon one more idea related to this context. Again it is easy to understand because you already have the domain knowledge.

If I want to predict someone's salary from only age assuming a linear relationship what am I losing? Is this model practical? Your answer will immediately be in the negative. This is because salary depends on many other variables too such as qualification, location, performance and the likes. When should you stop listing? You can make your model only as close to reality as possible but never real!

11. Predicting Fortunate/ Unfortunate Events

(Imagine that predictive model of X predicts that X is going to die soon. Would X like to be a good data scientist?)

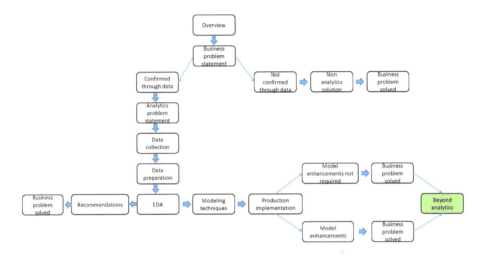

Can I predict death? I can use the sequence of millions of events that have occurred in a person's life until now and then predict which events are more likely to happen in the near future. Filter out the ones having death in them, and you have your prediction.

Let's say my model predicts that my friend is going to die on the 15th of June 2019. I run to him and alert him. We try to avert the danger, and he survives. Today is the 16th of June 2019. Was my model's prediction correct? Assuming my friend was going to die my prediction was spot on in the first place. But he has not died yet. How can I claim that the model did the right job? The only way to find out is not to publish the prediction of death to the friend. Allow 15th June to pass, friend to die and then claim to the rest of the world that my prediction was correct!

Instead, what if my prediction says that my friend is going to win a huge lottery on 15th June 2019. I run to my friend and declare to him the good news and both of us work towards making the prediction true (at the least buy a lottery ticket assuming he does not have a ticket yet).

This makes me think when we predict and publish an unfortunate event the tendency is to work towards invalidating the prediction. Real life model accuracy is hurt. However, when we predict and publish a fortunate event, there are high chances we will work towards making that happen. Real life model accuracy is boosted. If the prediction is not published, then over a couple of hundreds of such events, we get the actual accuracy of the model. In this case, I might be a good data scientist but a bad human being! Some food for thought. Isn't it?

12. Hop a Little, Jump a Little from Stage to Stage

(What is common among Kangaroo, Rabbit and Frog? They hop!)

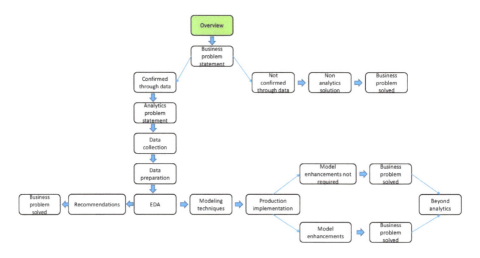

What are the steps or stages of a typical data science project? There could be a theoretical and ideal answer in various books. Don't forget the CRISP-DM either. However, I am not a big fan of this representation. My apologies to whoever came up with that. From the observation of my day to day work in analytics, I am going to mention the following steps.

1. Business Problem Definition

Understand the domain and understand what concern the business user has. Find out if the problem could be solved using analytics at all.

2. Conversion of Business Problem Statement to An Analytics Problem Statement

A business problem could have multiple analytics problems associated with it. Discuss with stakeholders as to which analytics problem could be chosen for a solution. One might have to estimate ROI, find out the feasibility of implementation, maintainability and robustness of solution at this stage for each analytics solution and rank order them. This will help make a decision. Given the fact that different solutions might benefit different departments in the organization, the data scientist may have to go ahead with more than one solution in parallel.

3. A Depiction of the Architecture of Analytics Solution on Paper

This is usually a technical diagram of source-to-inputs-to-models-to-output-to-destination. A single look at this will let an experienced data scientist validate the idea immediately.

4. Data Identification and Collection

One should determine what data to collect. In smaller teams, the data scientist usually collects the data by himself. Data could be collected from the warehouse or from other sources such as public internet domains or directly from business in the form of files.

5. Data Understanding and Preparation

Understand the business significance of each variable. Handle missing values. Handle outliers. Decide on a level and aggregate if necessary. This keeps the data ready for exploratory data analysis and modeling. I am not going into details of each topic here. We can talk whenever we meet next over the phone or in person.

6. Exploratory Data Analysis

Check summary statistics. Carry out univariate and bivariate analyses. Identify dependent and independent variables. Do variable importance analysis using Boruta or PCA. Come up with any insights that the data has to provide. Certain projects, the ones that don't require model building, stop here.

7. Modeling

Once the important and useful variables are found using the previous step, a supervised algorithm (a target label is present) or an unsupervised algorithm (no target label) is suitably applied on the data for the model to learn the pattern and apply it on new similar data to make informed decisions.

8. Model Testing

Compare train and test diagnostics. They should be close. Iterate model building process by changing input variables, by changing train-test split ratio, by changing modeling technique altogether, by including more historical data, by converting variable types from numeric to categorical and vice versa (if necessary), Cross Validation or any other enhancement technique that appears suitable to you.

9. Analytics Solution Demo to Stakeholders

Usually by this time a proof of concept is ready with approximate accuracies and expected results. Use soft skills such as visualization and presentation techniques to impress your stakeholders.

10. Productionalization of Analytics Solution

You have to enhance the PoC to a full-fledged solution that could be implemented in the production environment. Few things that one has to take care of are automatic data sourcing, automatic processing, automatic analytics output display for consumption by user and integration with the end system. This step takes a substantial amount of time. Come up with a prediction frequency.

11. Model Retraining

In most cases, you have to keep retraining the model with latest same-variable data at regular intervals. This protects the model from getting stale.

12. Accuracy Calculation in Production

Devise a way to automatically monitor predictions and accuracy calculations by comparing with real-life outcomes. If the performance of the model is not up to expectations, then use any of the model enhancement techniques.

There are a few things to keep in mind. The above steps are neither strictly sequential nor execute-only-once in nature. That's why you see the loop in CRISP-DM.

13. Passing on to Next Generation

(Knowledge is not like countries. It has no boundaries)

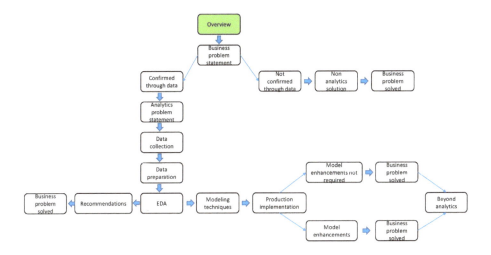

Keeping things in human memory is one of the easiest ways to retain them. Also, keeping things in memory is one of the most difficult ways to use it if memory fails. After you have successfully implemented an analytics project how do you describe it to your fellow data scientist who has just joined the team?

1. Context

2. Business problem statement

3. Analytics problem statement

4. Analytics solution approach

5. Technical design diagram of the analytics solution

6. Summary statistics

7. Performance evaluation

8. Road ahead

9. File naming convention

10. Input files

11. Code logic flow

12. Output files

13. Production implementation. Directories. Logs. Movement of files. Archiving. Scheduling. Notification. Integrating with existing IT tool.

14. Hardware and software requirements

15. Packages needed

16. Expected number of records and expected size of input files

17. Expected duration of run in development, test and production environments

18. Expected number of records and expected size of output files

19. Sample artifacts

However, this list could be subjective to the type of project you are working on. More or less you can revolve around the above topics.

14. Summarize Basic Modeling Techniques. Will You?

(One remains a student lifelong. So, study. A busy man always finds time. So, don't complain of being busy)

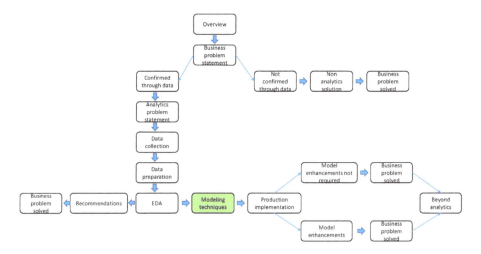

For each modeling technique, I will mention the learning method, nature of independent variable, nature of dependent variable, regression or classification, relevant algorithm and diagnostics.

Supervised – Class of learning where there is a target label present. For example, in email spam identification, there should be a label marked as "Spam" or "Not Spam" along with other variables for the model to learn the patterns.

Unsupervised – Class of learning where there is no target label present. For example, the grouping of customers by purchasing behavior. The machine learns through observations and finds structures in data.

Regression – Machine is trained to predict some value like price, weight or height. For example, predicting house price or stock price.

Classification – Machine is trained to classify something into some class. For example, classifying whether a subject has a disease or not.

Diagnostics – Process to check the performance of the model to identify the pain points and tune the model if required.

Linear Regression

1. Supervised

2. Continuous/Categorical independent variables

3. Continuous dependent variable

4. Regression

5. Ordinary Least Squares (OLS) algorithm

6. Diagnostics are R Square, adjusted R Square, MAPE, RMSE, residual scatter plot, constant error variance (homoscedasticity), the absence of multicollinearity, linearity between dependent and independent variables, Cook's distance and outliers

Logistic Regression

1. Supervised

2. Continuous/Categorical independent variables

3. Binomial categorical dependent variable

4. Classification

5. Maximum likelihood algorithm

6. Diagnostics are accuracy from confusion matrix, ROC curve, AUC, gains table and lift chart, KS statistic, concordant % and discordant %

Multinomial Logistic Regression

1. Supervised

2. Continuous/Categorical independent variables

3. Categorical dependent variable with more than two levels

4. Classification

5. Diagnostics are overall accuracy and class accuracy

Decision Tree

1. Supervised

2. Continuous/Categorical independent variables

3. Continuous/Categorical dependent variable

4. Regression/classification

5. Node splitting criteria are Gini index, chi-square, entropy and variance

6. Diagnostics are accuracy from confusion matrix for classification and RMSE for regression

Random Forest

1. Supervised

2. Continuous/Categorical independent variables

3. Continuous/Categorical binomial/ categorical multinomial dependent variable

4. Regression/classification

5. Node splitting criteria are Gini index, chi-square, entropy and variance. Uses bagging for multiple trees

6. Diagnostics are accuracy from confusion matrix for classification and RMSE for regression

Clustering

1. Unsupervised

2. No concept of independent or dependent variables

3. Not a regression or classification technique

4. Algorithms are K means and hierarchical

5. Diagnostics for K-means are strength, R square, WSS and BSS

6. Could be hard or fuzzy (probabilistic membership) clustering

Association Mining

1. Unsupervised

2. No concept of independent or dependent variables

3. Not a regression or classification technique

4. Apriori algorithm

5. Diagnostics are support, confidence and lift

6. Also called market basket analysis (MBA)

7. Input data is in the form of transactions

Time Series

1. A task for you. Find out if we can call it supervised learning because we are forecasting Y using previous values of Y. However, which one would you call the independent variable – Time or Y?

2. ARIMA is an example

3. For ARIMA: AIC and BIC are used to compare among models

Text Analytics

1. Supervised/Unsupervised method to identify patterns from textual data which is in the form of structured (tabular form) or unstructured (websites, social feeds).

2. Tokenization, Stop words removal, Parts of Speech Tagging, Stemming Lemmatization.

3. Document term matrix or any of its transformations is the input.

4. Diagnostic is accuracy in case of supervised learning.

There are a few more techniques that you should know.

- K Nearest Neighbor
- Naive Bayes
- Matrix Factorization
- Collaborative Filtering
- Survival Analysis
- PCA
- Factor Analysis
- Neural Networks

The task for you is to find out for them similar details as above.

15. Train and Test Datasets. Should They Be Twins?

(Do not build on apples and test on airplanes)

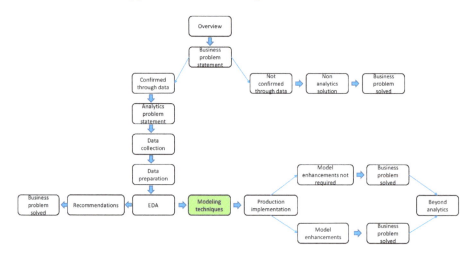

Imagine a situation where you are trying to determine the number of footfalls at your retail store. You want to personalize items based on age. One example of personalization is stocking more items preferred by the most frequent age group. Let's assume that your data scientist needs to build a statistical model to come up with recommendations. Don't worry about whether this is a modeling based analytics problem statement. Simply assume. He will train and test the model and compare the diagnostics specific to the modeling technique.

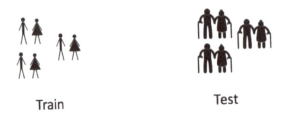

Train   Test

Profiles of Train and Test Datasets

Let's say that the train and test datasets look like the one in the picture above. A model that is trained on young customers will perform very poorly during a test where most of the customers are old.

This condition of good performance in train and bad in test often happens in data science and is usually called over-fitting. However, here we are more focused on a 'wide difference' in train and test accuracies because of non-similar profiles of train and test data.

This is when a methodology named 'Covariance Shift' comes into the picture. This is used to assess situations where predictor variables have different distributions in train and test data.

Measuring Covariance Shift

1. Combine both train and test data into a unified data.

2. Remove target variable.

3. Create a new variable which holds only two values (0 for train and 1 for test).

4. Using this new variable as target create a classification model.

5. AUC metric is used to estimate how much Covariance shift the data has

If AUC score is greater than 0.8, then there is an indication of strong Covariance shift between train and test. A good set of data (train and test) should ideally have a low covariance shift measure.

Ways of Reducing the Impact of High Covariance Shift

1. Dropping those features causing the shift.

2. Estimating density ratio of the probability of Test to Train and using that as weights to improve the observations which seem similar to test data.

I hope, now you have a better understanding of Covariance Shift and how to identify and treat accordingly.

16. What Should the Data Science Practitioner Be Careful About?

(In the hurdle race of data science, everyone is a winner because everyone completes)

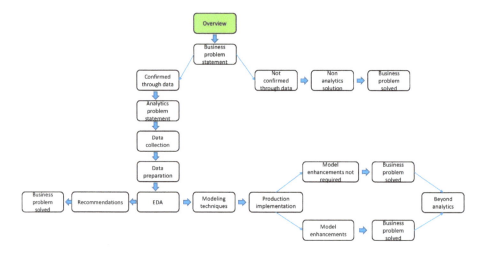

Business Head: I won't spend any money on analytics till you show me it's ROI.

Data Scientist: I can't show you ROI of analytics unless you agree to spend some money.

A circular problem just got created. This and many more challenges are faced by a data scientist each day. Here could be a helpful list.

1. Identifying opportunities for business problems that could be solved using analytics.

2. Sensitizing business teams on benefits of analytics so that they sponsor.

3. Bad quality of data with missing values, outliers and junk values.

4. Lack of completeness in the training data set. New levels of a categorical variable found in test or production data are not eligible for prediction.

5. Handling data with very low event rate such as detection of cancer, detection of fraudulent transactions.

6. Low volume of data available for analysis.

7. Ensuring the model clears all 7–10 diagnostics and deciding appropriate course of action in case of a diagnostic failure.

8. Agreeing on what level of performance of the model is acceptable.

9. Performance calculation in the live environment. I call it the real-life accuracy as against the technical accuracy.

10. Continuous profiling of inputs and outputs of the model and building a monitoring tool capable of sending alerts regularly.

11. Effort estimation.

12. Justifying failed efforts on experimenting with algorithms.

13. Proof of concept could be easy. Making the solution production ready requires lots of automation and carefulness.

14. Attributing a positive business outcome to an analytics solution.

15. Retraining model using new data captured after production implementation.

16. Enhancing model by various techniques such as the addition of new independent variables.

17. Handling a very high number of variables.

18. Consumption of output especially when analytics solution needs to be integrated into a tool owned by a different team.

19. Collecting relevant data.

20. Managing hardware and software requirements for handling a very high volume of data.

21. Special treatment necessary for handling unstructured data.

22. Handling categorical variables with a large number of levels. Google on how categorical variables are handled by statistical algorithms. Don't worry too much about continuous variables.

23. Assuming all business problems are analytics problems and hence forcing an analytics solution.

I know the list of challenges looks long. But don't worry. As data scientists, we are confident of overcoming all of them and taking the responsibility of adding value to businesses across domains and functions. Let's ride the wave together.

17. The Underplayed EDA

(I do not need a bald head to shine)

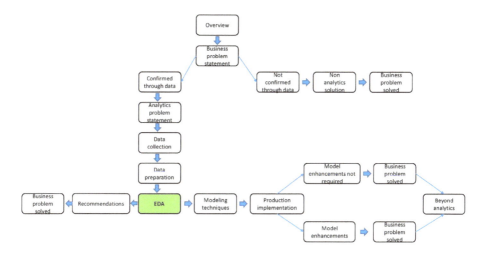

It takes more to keep things simple than to make them complex. It is of great significance in the data science world.

Exploratory Data Analysis, as the name suggests is exploring data and consequently finding insights. Many a time the learning derived from this exercise leads to an incredible impact on the business results. Needless to say that EDA is simpler and requires lesser effort than modeling. Hence, it is not wrong to imagine that many projects end at EDA output alone without relying on a predictive model.

Is it giving you a sense that only EDA or only modeling is used for any scenario? I am sorry. Modeling requires a good EDA as a prerequisite. It is not a mandatory technical requirement.

A diligently done EDA gives

- Summary statistics and hence a good understanding of the profile of data you are dealing with

- Understanding of a single variable

55

■ Understanding of the relationship between two variables

■ Visualization to represent the data

■ Useful insights for business decision making

Let's have a quick quiz. Assume that the nature of the two variables is the following. Tell me at least one EDA tool (graph/chart/table et cetera.) that can be used in the scenarios below.

■ Continuous/continuous (bivariate)

■ Continuous/categorical (bivariate)

■ Categorical/categorical (bivariate)

■ Continuous (univariate)

■ Categorical (univariate)

Answers

1. Scatter plot

2. A single chart having multiple boxplots

3. Cross-tabulation

4. Histogram, boxplot (I know you will wonder about the difference between histogram and bar chart because, after all, they look almost similar. Find out. Should I not be using a bar chart in a bivariate case?)

5. Frequency table or a bar chart

I want to name data scientists who specialize in discovering insights using EDA as data explorers or data detectives!

18. Role of Analytics in Psychiatric Disorders

(Mind plays a better role than analytics in psychiatric disorders. Obviously!)

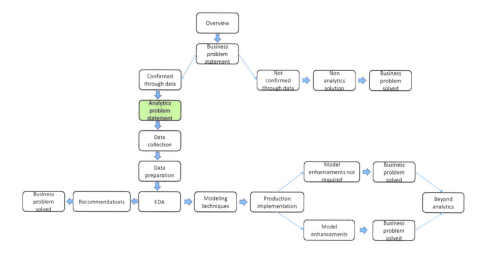

Mental health decides how people think, feel and behave in daily life.

It affects your ability to cope with stress, overcome challenges, and recover from life setbacks and hardships. Few of us would argue that mental health should be of low priority due to deadline policy that we work on. According to Psychological association, humans do not recognize the vulnerabilities of mental health issues until it starts to show up with health symptoms. By 2030, it is estimated that mental illness will surpass communicable disease which is quite alarming.

People with mental illness generally do not have a sense of contentment, the ability to laugh and have fun, the ability to deal with stress, a sense of meaning and purpose in activities and relationships, and balance between work and play. Identifying people with mental illnesses becomes even more tedious as they seldom try to come out in the open with such issues. With the advancements in technology, particularly in the area of data science, I strongly believe that we could come up with a framework which would monitor, analyze and predict the likelihood of people suffering from mental illness and would recommend prevention steps.

We know that Social Media has taken over today's generation and has kept them hooked on for prolonged hours. But nothing can beat the stress-busting and mood-boosting power of quality face to face time with other people. Analytics can be used in such cases and perhaps indicate users if they are hooked on to certain social media platform for beyond regular use. It can also be used to indicate some exercises for the eyes and hands to keep them more relaxed. It can also suggest people's proximity in real time so that they can meet each other in person instead of communicating via social media.

Not many will be aware, but the diet that we typically follow affects the way we think and feel. An unhealthy diet can take a toll on our brain and mood, disrupt our sleep and result in weakening our immune system. Food that adversely affects mood is caffeine, alcohol, trans-fat food, sugary snacks and refined carbs. Analytics can play a role in determining the acceptable range of consumption of these foods and can monitor individual intake and warn if it exceeds the acceptable limits. Analytics can also be used here to suggest alternative healthier diet options to people and track the well-being of a person. It can also be used as an obesity indicator, BMI tracker and can alert in case of any discrepancies.

We all lead a busy life and more often than not, we cut back on sleep to deliver our best. It may seem like a smart move but when it comes to your mental health, getting enough sleep is a necessity, not a luxury. Skipping even a few hours here and there can take a toll on your mood, energy, and mental sharpness. Analytics here can be used in monitoring the duration and pattern of sleep. It can also be used to track the snore patterns as it plays a key role in determining how tired we are. It can be used to detect patterns of body movement during sleep that can aid in deciding the extent of illness, if any.

19. Text Analytics in Its Deceivingly Innocent Form

(Now I know why we should not always judge a book by its cover)

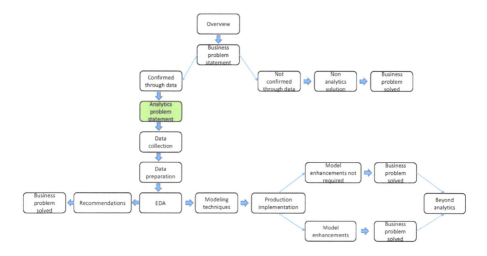

Feelings-to-text-to-feelings. The first half is always manual and requires the human being to express his feelings in the form of words either written or spoken. The second half relates to a machine to somehow understand and interpret the voice or text and feed a business user.

It is very evident that feelings to text conversion will have 100% accuracy as it is done by the human brain. The accuracy of the conversion from text to feelings, when done by a machine, is where the biggest challenge lies. I pat myself on the back if I get a 60–70% accuracy! Remember accuracy could be a train accuracy or test accuracy (which are technical accuracies) or a real-life accuracy determined by comparing with actual outcomes from decisions taken by believing in the statistical model.

Text analytics could be in the form of either unsupervised learning or supervised learning. Remember that here we are dealing with unstructured textual data. Our standard statistical modeling techniques are not capable of processing such data directly. So we convert unstructured data to structured data before feeding to the algorithm. An example of unsupervised learning is sentiment analysis and that of supervised learning is identifying spam SMSes. That was a tricky statement to make! Actually, any of the above two problem statements could serve as examples of both supervised and unsupervised learnings. Tell me how. A task for you!

Following is a list of steps a typical and simple supervised text analytics solution will have.

Train and Test

- Divide the data into train and test sets. Ensure you have similar profiles of the train and test sets (plan for having similar proportions of the Y label at the least)

Text Preprocessing on Train Data

- Transform the text into a corpus. A corpus is a collection of textual information combined from all sources into one single stack.

- Convert corpus to lower case to make it uniform across all textual information and not have separate representations for uppercase and lowercase.

- Remove numbers so that there is no importance given to non-alphabetic characters.

- Remove stop words or junk words which do not add meaning, punctuations and white spaces.

- Stem the words so that words in plural form are extracted back to root form to avoid redundancy. For example, running can be stemmed to run.

Document Term Matrix

- Document Term Matrix creates a numerical representation of the documents in our corpus.

- A corpus is just a collection of documents. With this "larger" bag of words, we can do more interesting analytics. It is easy to determine individual word counts for each document or all documents.

- We can now calculate aggregates and basic statistics such as average term count, mean, median, mode, variance and standard deviation of the length of the documents.

- We can also tell which terms are more frequent in the collection of documents and can use that information to determine which terms more likely "represent" the document.

Build Model and Predict

- Build the model (example random forest) using the DTM of train data.

- Carry out text preprocessing on the test data. Apply the dictionary of train bag of words on the test data. After all, this is the only way you can predict on the test data using the trained model.

- Predict on test data and measure accuracy.

Tradeoff between Information Loss and Volume of Data

In the pursuit of keeping the volume of data manageable, we try to lose the unimportant information. Single casing, removal of numbers, stop words, punctuations and white spaces potentially cause loss of meaning from a text. Imagine somebody using block letters in a chat conversation to sound angry. Another person using exclamation marks to sound surprised. Sarcasm. But we agree to live with that to get the algorithm going. Note that with higher processing capacities these days we might not need to compromise.

I would have touched hardly 10% of the vast field of text analytics in this article. My suggestion for you is to self-study until I learn, apply and come back with more. Also, google for Natural Language Processing (NLP).

20. Predict Using Clustering. Really?

(Supervision does not always lead to the best results)

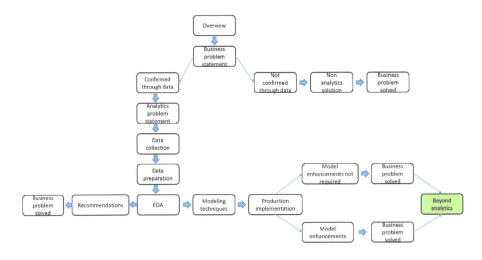

I came across a CV as part of an interview where one project was titled prediction but had details of clustering under it. The candidate realized and admitted that it was a typing mistake. That got me thinking. We can actually use clustering to aid prediction. Prediction is a typical skill of supervised learning.

There are three ways. First way – cluster the data. Build a separate classifier for each cluster. Second way – use the cluster identifier as a new categorical independent variable. Both these approaches are known to enhance the accuracy of the prediction. A little work for you. Find out which one is better. Wait. Are they the same?

The third way – this is something I would like to discuss somewhat elaborately. Let's say I have a cat who has an obsessive compulsive disorder (OCD). She jumps at 11 p.m. every day depending on certain conditions – the average temperature of the day, amount of rainfall, average humidity, and quantity of milk in the house. Jump/no jump is our variable of study.

We build four clusters based on historical data. Let's assume that cluster A has an 80–20 split of jump/no jump. Cluster B has 70–30. Cluster C has 25–75. Cluster D has 10–90. The question is that using these clusters can we predict at 4 p.m. every day whether the cat is going to jump in the night? Be watchful. We are demanding prediction from an unsupervised learning method.

A new day comes, and it is 4 p.m. We acquire the average temperature, total rainfall, average humidity and quantity of milk at that instant. We have devised a way to determine which cluster the day falls into by comparing the profiles of clusters with today's attributes. Assuming it falls into cluster B, we can safely predict that the cat is going to jump today (70% chance). If the day falls into cluster D, then there is a 90% chance that the cat will not jump today. That's our prediction.

What is the extent of approximation we are doing here? First, mapping the new day into a cluster. Second, none of our clusters is 100% pure. By the way, is no one worried about the poor cat's health?

21. What Is So Deep About Deep Learning?

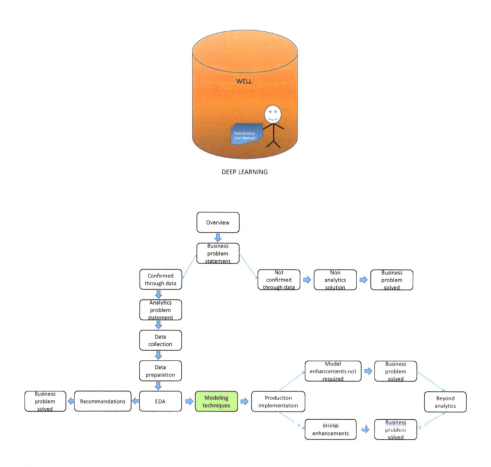

Remember the time when you rode a bicycle for the first time? By simply looking at it, you knew it had a handle, a seat, two wheels with spokes and pedals. Under the supervision of parents/elders, you were taught how to balance the body, how to manoeuvre, how to pedal and adjust speed accordingly. The countless falls and the constant supervision were necessary for you to learn from the mistakes during riding. You improved each time until one fine day when you could manage riding all by yourself.

This is the underlying concept on which Deep Learning works because after all, Deep Learning is an algorithm inspired by how the human brain functions.

Similar to how we learn from experience and practice, the deep learning algorithms would be trained on a task repeatedly, each time adjusting and correcting itself a little to improve the outcome. We call it 'deep learning' because both the natural and the statistical neural networks have various layers hidden that enable learning. Any problem displaying high complexity and requiring deep thought to figure out, is a problem where deep learning solutions can be applied.

They train on a set of input-output pairs and learn to model the pattern by updating the weights and biases of the model to minimize error. The error itself can be measured in a variety of ways including root mean squared error (RMSE).

Feedforward networks are like a game of guesses and responses. Each guess is a test of what we think we know, and each response is feedback letting us know how wrong we are.

In the forward pass, the signal flow moves from the input layer through the hidden layers to the output layer. The outcome of the output layer is measured against the actual true labels.

In the backward pass, using backpropagation, partial derivatives of the error function with respect to the various weights and biases are back-propagated through the Multilayer Perceptrons (MLP). That act of differentiation gives us a gradient or a landscape of error, along which the parameters may be adjusted. They move the MLP one step closer to the minimum error. This can be done with any gradient-based optimization algorithm such as stochastic gradient descent (taking each training data at one instance). The network keeps playing that game of guesses and responses until the error can't go any lower. This state is known as convergence.

Deep learning allows machines to solve complex problems even when using a data set that is very diverse, unstructured and inter-connected. The more deep learning algorithms learn, the better they perform. There are many flavors to this like Convolutional Neural Nets, Recurrent Neural Nets, Boltzmann Machines, Gated Recurrent Units, and Word2Vec that you can experiment on and get your hands dirty with.

22. Survival Analysis

(It is no more survival of fittest. It's survival of the one who adapts the best.)

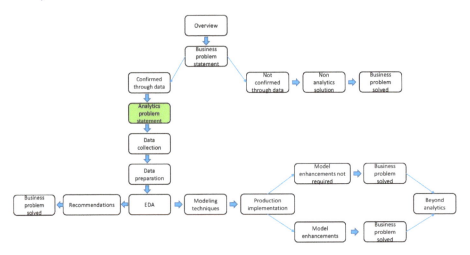

If you are a 90's kid, the chances are high that you would have encountered one particular viral feed on social media platforms couple of years ago that gives you the date of death given your name as input. That was absurd and illogical but at the same time fun to share with peers. But, what if I tell you that now with the advancements in Data Science, there is a statistical method for predicting how long you or anything would survive. Welcome to the concept of Survival Analysis.

Survival Analysis is used for analyzing the duration of time until an event occurs. An event here could be anything ranging from machine component failure, policy lapse to death of living organisms, next purchase by a customer and so on. It can be applied in cases where there is a "lifetime" factor involved.

Following terms are often associated during modeling using Survival Analysis:

1. **Event** – Any occurrence of interest such as mechanical failure, diagnosis of disease, death, customer churn. It can be a one-off event

66

such as death or a recurring event such as machine component failure.

2. **Time** – Period of study.

3. **Censored** – Instances where there was no event recorded across the entire period or instances where there was a cut-off during the period of study. For example, missing information of a machine during the study of its lifetime or cases of patients withdrawing abruptly in the middle of disease control study.

4. **Survival Function** – Probability of survival longer than the given time.

5. **Hazard Function** – Probability of an event occurring after it has survived longer than the given time.

Survival analysis can be used in several ways.

1. To describe the survival times of members of a single group using Kaplan-Meier curves.

2. To compare the survival times of two or more groups using the log-rank test.

3. To describe the effect of categorical or quantitative variables on survival using Cox proportional-hazards regression.

Let us understand more with an example of a use case. Assume you are the head of the Hiring team who has a limited number of job offers to roll out to talented candidates. You have been targeting potential candidates with this offer for the past one year. Now you want to learn from the past behavior of the recruitment process and target candidates who are likely to join the organization.

You will have to use survival analysis in this case because the dependent variable is the time taken before the candidate joins the organization. It also contains censored data which are candidates who did not join the organization till date after accepting the offer.

The objective to start a discussion on survival analysis here is not restricted to only this technique. I hope this article gives you the understanding to explore various other use cases where survival analysis can be used.

23. A Customized Ensemble Model

(Being together is better than being alone)

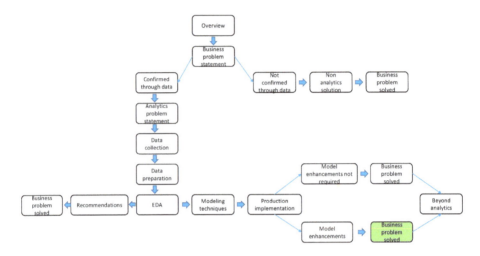

A talking cat visits her family doctor. The doctor is supposed to diagnose what disease the cat is suffering from out of a standard set of ten diseases. Following are the attributes/factors which the doctor can use to identify the illness. Body temperature, hair color, stomach pain (yes/no), nausea (yes/no), age, gender and a piece of textual information on the cat's lifestyle. The text could contain a description of how the cat drinks milk, goes to the gym, drives a car and leads a sedentary occupation.

So there are six structured attributes and one unstructured attribute. We can solve this problem with a single model version or an ensemble version.

In the single model approach, we want to convert the textual column into multiple structured columns. Identify key terminologies. Create a new categorical column for each term and assign present/absent for each historical record. Remember that we already have the disease name in each record. Build a model using multinomial logistic regression or random forest and you are done.

Can I make the solution a little smarter? Do I mean complex! Let's separate the structured attributes and unstructured attribute into two different models – model 1 and model 2.

Two scenarios could happen during prediction. Model 1 and model 2 give us the same disease or different diseases. When it is the same disease, we are confident about our diagnosis. The problem happens when they predict two different diseases. Shall we believe model1 which is built on structured data or believe model 2 which is built on unstructured data?

The beauty is that we can make that decision data based. On the historical data get model1 prediction and model 2 prediction. We already have the actual disease name because data is historical. Find out instances where model1 wins and where model 2 wins. There might be cases where neither of them got the correct disease, or both of them got it. In cases of neither we decide to pick model1 and for both we pick model 2. I know you will argue. This only proves that data science is as much an art as it is a science!

Introduce a new dependent variable – 'choice' having two possible values model1 and model 2. Create a train dataset with all structured and unstructured attributes as input and choice as the output. Build the model and call it model 3.

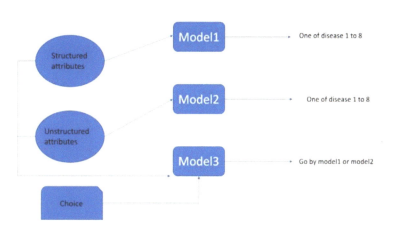

Pictorial Representation of the Analytics Solution

Whenever the next talking cat comes, predict using model 1, predict using model 2, determine using model 3 which prediction you should go with. I am not sure yet why I am always behind cats!

24. Machining Machine Learning

(What is it like to automate automated systems?)

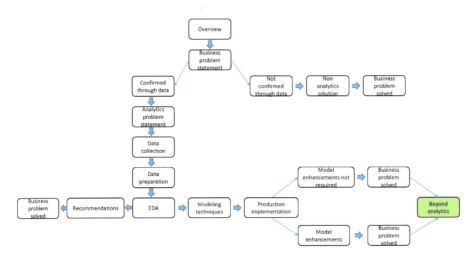

As if the machine learning, in itself, was not enough machine-like I went ahead and thought of a way to automate the complete machine learning process. I will talk about what all features would be required to make the package useful. A lot more consideration is needed to develop and implement it.

Data Preparation

The data preparation module should produce the following automatically as soon as the raw dataset is provided as input

- Summary statistics.

- Number of continuous variables and number of categorical variables.

- Missing-ness map showing the spread of missing values.

- Remove variables having more than 30% (just saying. Decide for yourself) missing values.

70

- Remove all records having missing values.

- Develop a strategy for elimination versus imputation.

- For continuous variables replace missing values with the average value. For categorical variables, you can just replace with the mode.

- Regenerate summary statistics.

Exploratory Data Analysis

This module takes the prepared data set and creates the following

- Univariate analysis.

  1. For a continuous variable generate a histogram and a boxplot. Have a strategy for binning if necessary. 2) For a categorical variable come up with a frequency of occurrence of each value, list and number of distinct values and strategy for binning if necessary. 3) Generate takeaways from the univariate analysis.

- Bivariate analysis.

  1. Concentrate on all possible pairs 2) Generate scatter plots for continuous/continuous pairs 3) Generate boxplots having multiple boxes in one chart for continuous/categorical pairs 4) Do cross-tabulations for categorical/categorical pairs 5) Generate semi-insights for each relationship.

Modeling

Identify whether your problem statement can be solved by supervised learning. If yes then from the dependent variable one can determine to go either the regression way or classification way. Again the dependent variable will tell us whether we are dealing with binomial or multinomial classification. Allow the user to input the train/test distribution numbers.

Build and test the following models for *regression* technique.

- *Linear Regression*. Pick up SLR/MLR based on the number of independent variables.

- Create a model evaluation strategy. The strategy will be carried forward to other modeling techniques too.

- Strategy: 1) Display all diagnostics 2) Comment on over-fitting 3) Plot bias/variance and choose the optimum point 4) Arrive at an overall diagnostic score 5) Combine train/test datasets and rebuild model 6) Finally generate semi insights.

- Build *regression decision tree* and apply the model evaluation strategy.

- Build *a regression random forest* and apply the model evaluation strategy.

- Come up with a comparison chart or table for all of the above regression techniques.

- Recommend data scientist to go with the best one.

Build and test the following models for *binomial classification* and apply model evaluation strategy to all.

- Logistic regression

- Classification decision tree

- Classification random forest

- Naive Bayes

- KNN

- SVM

- Neural networks

- Comparison chart among all techniques

- Recommend the best one

Build and test the following models for *multinomial classification* and apply model evaluation strategy to all.

- Multinomial logistic regression.

- Random forest.

- Comparison chart between the two.

- Pick the best one.

Clustering

For the moment let's keep hierarchical aside and go ahead with K-means and K-prototype clustering.

- Take all numeric variables as input.

- Determine the optimum number of clusters using elbow curve.

- Build K-means and K-Prototype clusters. Do keep in mind that the former technique uses only numeric variables while the latter can deal with a combination of numeric and categorical variables.

- Compare diagnostics and choose the better model.

Association Mining

- Use the Apriori algorithm.

- Give transactions data set as input.

- Create diagnostics using support, confidence and lift.

- Choose top rules.

- Generate semi-insights.

Time Series Modeling

- Check for stationarity of series.

- Use the ARIMA modeling technique.

- Build models with varying values of p, d, q.

- Pick up the best one.

- Predict using the chosen model.

Deployment

Production deployment will happen with manual intervention.

Performance

Have a strategy for calculating real life accuracies and overall performance in the live environment.

Retraining

- With additional recent records created from usage.

- With additional variables captured.

- Repeat real-life performance measurement.

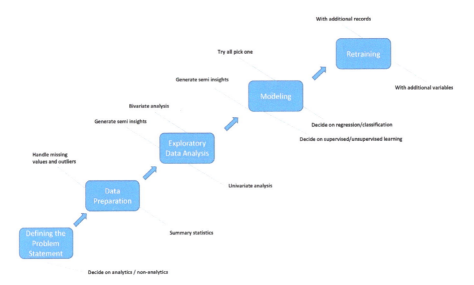

Features of Automation of the Analytics Process

The intention of this article is not to provide you with a solution of automation but to get you thinking on these lines. With this are you reducing the art component and increasing the science component of analytics? The thought of a machine and a data scientist working hand in hand to solve problems of humankind makes me look forward to the future with excitement.

25. Can Machine Learning Replace Its Master, the Data Scientist?

(Man versus machine has remained an unresolved debate)

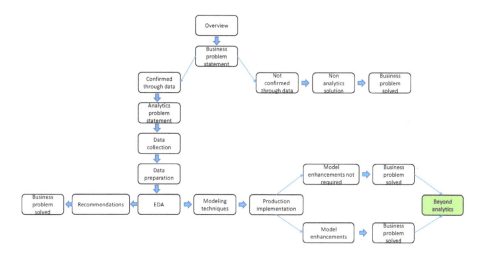

Artificial Intelligence is empowering more machine intelligence embedded in human systems than ever before. We might even call this intrusion of the algorithm an epidemic on the social organization.

We suspect that its impact will be progressive and profound on all human activity and a multitude of professional tasks.

Advances in deep learning and areas of AI will coincide with the rise of smarter robots. A set of AI machines by the company Alibaba recently became the first to beat a human at a reading comprehension test. We didn't expect to see AI beat human experts at Go or Jeopardy in the same decade. So much is the hype surrounding AI.

Many machine learning vendors, ranging from Google to startups like Data-robot and H_2O. AI, claim that they can automate machine learning. That sounds great! Then you, the hiring manager, won't need to go chasing after data science talent whose skills you can't judge in a bidding war you can't win. You'll automate all those skills away.

However, the skills that data scientists possess are hard to automate, and people who seek to buy automated AI should be aware of what exactly can be automated, and what can't, with present technology. Data scientists perform many tasks. While automating some of those tasks may lighten their workload, unless you can automate all of their functions, they are still necessary, and that rare talent will remain a choke point that hinders the implementation of machine learning in many organizations.

A few tasks in a larger data science workflow can be automated. A few happy paths through the complexity can be traced using automation. But for custom solutions, data scientists are still necessary. If you compare it to a kitchen, automated ML is like a robot that knows how to flip dosas. You still need a cook on the line, even if you're saving them some time.

Automated ML is like automation of automation. The practice of machine learning comes down to two main tasks in the core of automated machine learning which are

1. Automated optimization of feature engineering and feature selection.

2. Hyperparameter tuning.

Some aspects of data science are more difficult to automate such as statistical testing, communicating with stakeholders, domain knowledge, formulating data-based policies, et cetera. That is why "data science" cannot be fully automated. There is a difference between automating the entire process and automating the tools used within the process. Human involvement, for the foreseeable future, is paramount, not only for overseeing and correcting course for any level of automation but also to kick off searches for idea generation. We may be able to automate exploratory investigations, but the human element will need to make careful decisions on which courses of action are worthy of pursuit.

Artificial intelligence may eliminate some jobs but it will also create new ones, and work that is done by humans will be more thoughtful, rewarding and fulfilling. AI will make us beyond human, in effect, superhuman.

26. Can Models Mimic Reality?

(One imperfect model is better than no model)

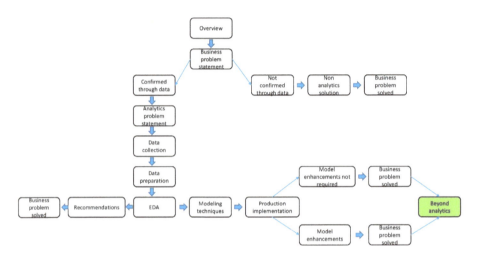

Can a predictive model mimic reality? Can there be a perfect model which never goes wrong? Imagine a model recommending a decision to a sales head in an organization. How frequently should the sales head go with the recommendation? Let's think about one data point in history which was used to build the model. It corresponds to a decision A which he had taken in an instance when his mood was terrible. Otherwise, he would have ideally taken decision B. There are chances that this data point will appear as an outlier and you might decide to do away with the data point. What happens if the sales head's mood goes bad quite often. It would make sense to, somehow, include the decision maker's mood as a variable. The inclusion of mood would implicitly take care of other variables which impact mood such as surrounding temperature, lighting, humidity, latest conversation with family, friends and colleagues, bank balance, physical and mental health, hours of sleep, et cetera.

Why stop at mood? How about intention? In our models, we assume that the sales head wishes to take a rational decision. What if he is serving his notice period with the organization, has gone crazy and wants the organization to fare poorly in business at least to the extent he can impact. This means I should have captured mood and intention as two different input variables for the model and should determine mood and intention before prediction.

What is the stopping criterion? Making the model too complex with too many variables will result in high variance and hence high total error (google for the bias-variance tradeoff in statistical model building and let me know what you understand).

27. When the Data Scientist in Me Becomes a Philosopher

(Where there is science there is philosophy too)

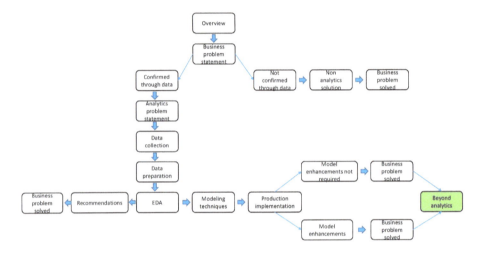

I see philosophy in many things. I look for philosophy in many things. I see because I look for it. Data science is a no different wonder for me.

Few quick thoughts. Believe at your own risk.

1. You cannot predict the future away. You will have to live it.

2. I walked into a random forest and lost my way.

3. I met linear regression and became a data scientist. I met neural networks and became a deep learner.

4. Whenever a model is angry and throws absurd accuracies, don't forget to thank it. It only wants the best out of you.

5. R to a data scientist: There are 99 reasons that you would not like me. But there is only one for which you will. I promise to wait for lifelong until you find that one reason.

6. A model with 99% accuracy is worse than a model with 10% accuracy if historical outcomes were bad.

7. No bad model is purely bad. At the least, it teaches us how not to build a model.

8. Prediction doesn't reduce uncertainty. Instead, it increases uncertainty by one unit by making us ask whether we should or shouldn't believe in the prediction.

28. Are You Too Generic or Too Specific? The Bias-Variance Tradeoff

(Tradeoff induces subjectivity which in turn induces art in a data scientist)

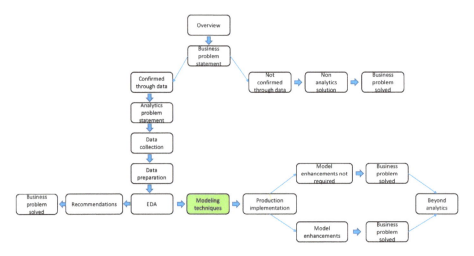

The bias-variance tradeoff is pivotal for arriving at an optimally performing supervised learning model. I intend to keep things simple here.

Bias is the difference between the average prediction of a model and the actual value. Model with high bias oversimplifies the model and pays little attention to train data points thereby leading to high approximations and hence high errors on train and test datasets. Variance, on the other hand, is a measure of how well spread the data is. It pays a lot of attention to train data points but does poorly on the data which it has never seen. So, which one is better? Neither. Both are errors. When we add up the bias and variance, we get a total error. And what is the way to play along the bias-variance tradeoff space? Increase or decrease the complexity of the model. If your question is how to recognize a complex model, then try adding an insane number of independent variables or try increasing depth of a decision tree to 30 levels.

In other words, bias represents how unfair something is with respect to others and variance represents how likely some things change with respect to others. Let us take an example of two cats discussing whether they should drink milk assuming that they can drink milk only when the baby alone is around in the house.

The first cat asks the second one whether they should drink the milk when

Scenario 1) only baby is around.

Scenario 2) only dad is around.

Scenario 3) only mom is around.

If the second cat answers 'yes' to all three scenarios then we can say that she is more biased towards drinking milk irrespective of who is there in the house. The accuracy is very poor in this case which 1/3 is. This is a classic case of high bias with a high chance of underfitting.

If the second cat answers 'yes' to scenario one alone, that means she is following the assumption condition cent percent and that she has learned the correct answer so much so that if you twist and ask her a question such as 'Can we drink milk when baby sister is around?', her answer might as well be in the negative. This is a classic case of high variance with a high chance of overfitting where there is no generalization.

I will stop here and leave the understanding of the decision trees depicted below to you assuming they are self-explanatory.

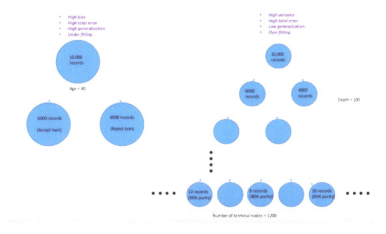

Pictorial Depiction of Bias and Variance

29. When Can Data Science Fail?

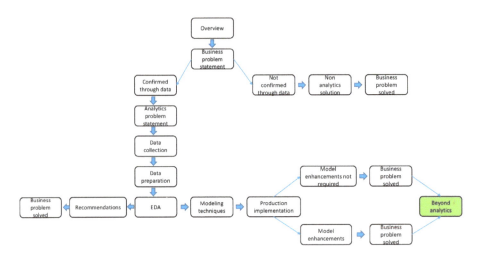

Needless to say that prediction in data science is an intelligent generalization and calculated specialization. The sweet spot in a model performance lies somewhere in between the two extremes of generalization and specialization.

Prediction fails when training of the model becomes too generic or too specific. In the former scenario, the model learns only little from the historical data while in the latter scenario, it learns a bit too much. Both arc harmful.

A less than proper sampling of the data for building our model produces inaccurate results during prediction. When the chosen sample is not a decent representation of the population, it doesn't do justice to the model we have trained and hence falls short.

Assuming that everything in nature and all human behavior could be modeled from historical data is, in my opinion, undermining the uniqueness of nature. Not every influencer could be captured and accommodated in a model. Not all events, natural or human-made, occur at a frequency conducive for a model building exercise.

A blind belief on recommendations from a model and lack of confidence on your intuition, feelings and experience might put you into trouble. There could always be a fear of handing over critical decision making to machines.

Organizations capture a variety of data related to their customer's demography or behavior. There is often a thin line separating right to privacy and intrusion. Who regulates that the insights generated from such data are used ethically.

A final thought. Who takes accountability of a wrong decision taken based on a machine's recommendation – data scientist? CIO? CEO?

I feel it's essential for us to understand both sides of the game, though as a data scientist, I am looking forward to the future with excitement. I will leave you here.

30. Data Science Interviews

(Asking questions is as challenging as answering them)

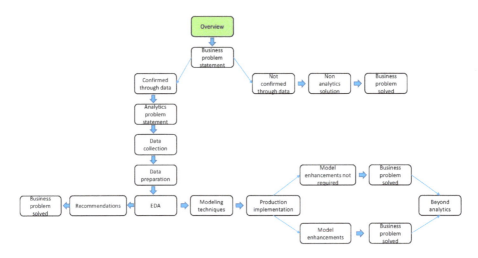

Tell me something about yourself. Why do you want to switch to data science? Do you have hands-on experience? We want managers who could also code having qualifications in statistics, analytics and management. There are very high chances that you will face these typical questions in an analytics interview. Do they make you comfortable or anxious?

Being in the data science technical panel for nearly six years has provided me with a wealth of knowledge on how I would like my interviews to be. However, you are free to express your disagreement.

Discussion

An interview is not an interrogation session. It is instead a discussion between two individuals evaluating how successful the relationship will be between the candidate and the organization. After all, it's a promise that they will help each other grow symbiotically. This prompts me to avoid giving you anything on lines of interviewer's points of view versus candidate's points of view.

Clarity on Expectations

The organization should be clear on what role and responsibility the candidate is being considered for. I am mentioning this specifically because I believe not all organizations are well versed with the analytics terminologies and hence with naming roles and designations. A data scientist is one who can work on a problem statement end to end starting from data collection and preparation to visualization and presentation to stakeholders. There are further specializations such as data explorers, machine learning experts and visualization experts. Quite often there are gaps between role available and evaluation carried out mainly because of lack of clarity on what means what. Please disagree if you are not with me.

EDA versus Modeling

There is a misconception that data science is modeling alone. This undermines the importance of insight generation from data exploration. Quite often by choosing the right exploration techniques one can discover deep insights which could impact business positively. A well-played EDA adds a lot of value to modeling too.

Threshold for Acceptable Performance

What level of performance of the candidate is acceptable? Since data science is an emerging technology, not many experts will be available at this point. How many instances of incorrect understanding are allowed?

Attitude

Attitude matters. Someone who is not very well versed with all analytics techniques but displays enthusiasm to explore, learn and delivery will be a better consideration than a mister know-all having a negative outlook towards life and growth.

Impressions

What did the candidate come across as in that one hour? Don't forget to focus on the importance of how the organization came across through the interviewer in that one hour. Every word the interviewer speaks is, in effect, on behalf of the organization.

Honesty

Honesty is golden. Honesty impresses me easily. It is always better to admit that you don't know something than beating around the bush. At least disclaim that you are not sure and hence guessing.

Missing Link Questions

I look for traits through which the candidate can move forward and arrive at the answer in response to missing link questions (created the phrase 'missing link questions' just now!)

Concept versus Application

Another attribute I look for is how many times during his analytics career has he asked WHY. That brings out vividly the difference between concept and mere application.

Communication

A well-built solution with not-so-effective communication is a loss. Imperfectly built solution with fantastic communication is also a loss. On this day we need the best of both worlds.

31. In Data Science There Is a Beginning but No End

(Whatever has a beginning has an end. Data Science, are you listening?)

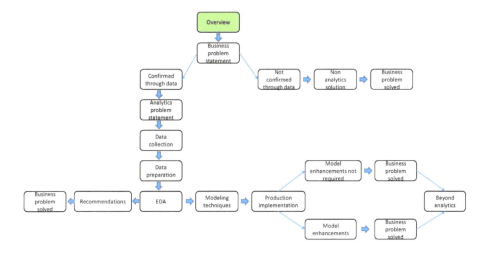

Many data science enthusiasts approach me asking for advice on where to start and what to learn. I have already answered all of them. However, here I am planning to give a structure to the response. I am going to list down few (only if you agree that these are few) things that are essential for someone to explore.

Introduction to Data Science

- What is data science?

- BI and data science

- Data science framework

- Acquire, prepare, analyze and act

- CRISP-DM

- The data science solution
- Types of data
- Examples of DS problem statements
- Data science maturity
- What makes a good data scientist?

Introduction to R

- Basic commands in R
- Advanced commands in R

Data Preparation and Exploratory Data Analysis

- Variable identification
- Missing value treatment
- Outlier treatment
- Skewness
- Univariate analysis
- Bivariate analysis
- Insight generation

Modeling

- Why modeling?
- What is a model?
- Supervised and unsupervised learning
- Regression and classification
- Dependent and independent variables
- Correlation and regression
- Train and test data

Linear Regression

- Simple linear regression
- Multiple linear regression
- Estimating regression coefficients
- Diagnostics and assumptions
- Stepwise linear regression
- Predicting using model

Logistic Regression

- Building the model
- Nature of the dependent variable
- Linear versus logistic regression
- Diagnostics – confusion matrix, accuracy, ROC, AUC, gains table, lift chart, KS statistic, concordance/discordance and F score

Multinomial Logistic Regression

- Nature of the dependent variable
- Building the model
- Diagnostics

Decision Tree

- Splitting nodes
- Terminologies
- Attribute selection criteria
- Gini index, information gain, reduction in variance and chi-square
- Pruning
- Regression and classification trees
- Diagnostics

Random Forest

- How is it different from individual decision trees?
- Diagnostics
- Handling multinomial dependent variable
- Bagging

Clustering

- Hard and soft clustering
- Algorithms – k means and hierarchical
- The optimum number of clusters and the optimum size of clusters
- Profiling clusters
- Diagnostics – WSS, BSS, Strength, R square
- Using clustering in supervised learning to enhance the accuracy

Time Series

- Why time series?
- Descriptive statistics
- Stationary and non-stationary series
- Components of time series
- ACF and PACF
- Autoregression and moving average
- ARIMA

Association Mining

- When is it used?
- Transactions
- Rules

- Item set
- Support, confidence and lift
- Apriori algorithm

Text Analytics

- Steps involved in a typical text analytics project
- Sentiment analysis
- Classification

Big Data

- Why and when?
- Overview
- Scale and challenges
- Hadoop ecosystem
- Big data analytics
- Spark, Pyspark and SparkR

Phew! Should I still assume that this is for beginners?

32. My Choice My Outcome

(If outcomes depend so heavily on choices why don't we focus on choices instead of outcomes?)

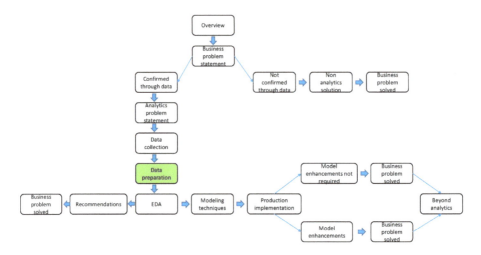

Garbage in Garbage out. Often it is said of machines that what you feed in is what you get. In the case of data analytics, it is no different. One might have to moderate their interpretation a bit. It is not often that you get to decide the quality of input data. Data preparation activities such as outlier handling, missing value treatment and aggregation are very handy when data in the raw form is not usable. Immediately a trade-off floods my mind. How much preparatory modifications can we accommodate while trying not to lose original information hidden in the data profoundly?

Early on while learning data science, it was inspiring to set off on an ambitious journey to predict defects using multiple linear regression. It seemed the most obvious problem to solve. But when we started gathering data for the analytics exercise, we realized there were many challenges. The biggest one was from the fact that organizations didn't capture and store the kind of data needed.

Soon we realized the data search exercise was in vain. How do we go about a data analytics activity without the right set of data points? Presence and nature of data challenge the choices we make in data exploration and model building.

The quest could have been the other way around. Organizations have a given set of data points. What business questions could we possibly answer through analytics? But is this the right way? It's your playground. You decide. Should we nudge organizations to capture additional data points that seem to help our objective better? Capturing new data points might take some time before a certain level of maturity is achieved.

33. Un-bias to Un-create

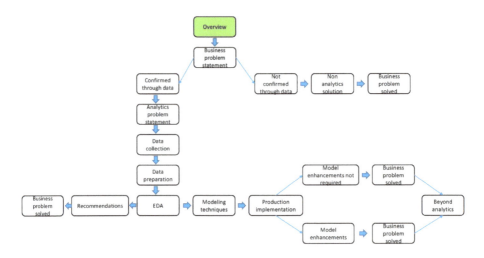

So much time is spent with data that it is only natural that we love the models we build so very passionately. In the war of modeling accurate outcomes, we lose sight of the constraints we build upon. There is enough discussion about how our inherent biases seep into the models we build.

Let's take some time to familiarize ourselves with biases. You are particularly keen about a car – a bright red one at that. And let me warn you that for the next few days or weeks may be, you would spot the very same model, make of car where ever you go. Most often it would appear in the same bright red color. You start to believe how popular this particular car is. No wonder you were right in shortlisting it. This is Confirmation Bias. Your beliefs are re-confirmed by what you keep seeing. What you don't realize is that you want to spot just that particular car, no matter what other information is presented to your brain. It is very easy to fall in this trap when one models an outcome.

Explore other cognitive biases at play. A very thought-provoking example that illustrates one such bias is Monkey Business Illusion. To get the best experience, do not ask anyone for feedback about it, or read any reviews or comments. Just watch the video that barely takes 2 minutes.

To a great extent, biases exist because of our preset notions about the world of data around us. Let us say that we are trying to decide what products should a particular pizzeria and burger shop sell. They are a reasonably large franchise. So far all their stalls are set near a stadium where matches happen regularly or in food courts. If the new store with an upgraded menu is to be established near a hospital, a primary school, an office complex, juxtaposed with a nutri-fit store or next to a pet shop, then none of the existing historical data gives us the right data points. This seemed an obvious example. But maybe it is not. Our model building approach heavily relies on existing knowledge.

No single solution fixes all our biases or pre-existing ideas. It needs a conscious effort to be aware of such cognitive biases and other preconceived notions that wield their way into the problem-solving approach. We should persistently question ourselves when we build models. And never shy away from discarding a model we developed if it does not solve the purpose.

34. No Negative Marks for Asking

(I just asked!)

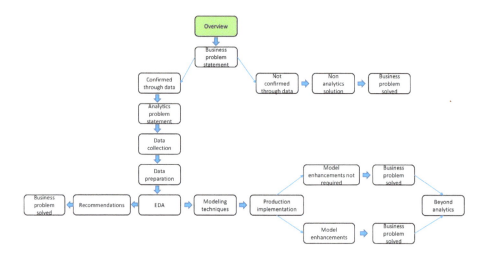

1. Is analytics worth the investment?

2. What is the difference between data science, analytics and machine learning?

3. Which one is more important – Exploratory Data Analysis or Modeling?

4. What is the difference between a business problem statement and an analytics problem statement?

5. What kind of problems cannot be solved using analytics?

6. What is a data set? What are observations and features?

7. What is the difference between dependent and independent variables?

8. Are histogram and bar chart the same?

9. Name a few activities that we do during data preparation?

10. What are the various EDA techniques available?

11. Is modeling mandatory for solving an analytics problem?

12. What kind of analytics can be done in the airline industry?

13. Explain Univariate, Bivariate and Multivariate analysis.

14. Is there a way to represent three categorical variables in a chart?

15. How does PCA work? Can we use that to show the importance of variables?

16. When is ANOVA preferred?

17. Explain Inferential and Descriptive Statistics.

18. What is Type 1 and Type 2 error?

19. Can we perform modeling on a data distribution which is not normal?

20. Which stage is more important, Data preparation or Data Modelling?

21. What are the challenges in data collection?

22. Which is better – R or Python or SAS?

23. What are the advantages and disadvantages of a GUI based analytics tool?

24. What are the assumptions of linear regression? If they are assumptions then why do we carry them out after building the model?

25. We check for the existence of outliers before building the linear regression model. Why do we check for outliers after model building too?

26. What is supervised and unsupervised learning? Give examples.

27. Is time series modeling supervised learning?

28. Is text analytics supervised or unsupervised learning?

29. What is the difference between regression and classification techniques?

30. What is the difference between correlation and regression?

31. What are the diagnostics of a linear regression model?

32. What are inputs/features/independent variables/predictors and outputs/dependent variable/predicted variables.

33. What is the difference between feature engineering, feature selection and dimension reduction?

34. Name a few regression and few classification modeling techniques.

35. What do you mean by generalization and specialization in machine learning techniques?

36. Explain bias/variance trade-off?

37. When do we say that a model is complex?

38. What are over-fitting and under-fitting problems?

39. Explain generalization and specialization concerning decision trees.

40. What are the diagnostics of logistic regression?

41. If logistic regression is a classification technique why is it named regression?

42. What all evaluations does a confusion matrix help with?

43. Which techniques are used for predicting a multinomial dependent variable?

44. What are the diagnostics of a model having a multinomial dependent variable?

45. What is a ROC curve? What are its X and Y axes?

46. What is a sweet spot on the ROC curve?

47. What is AUC?

48. How would you differentiate between good and bad ROC curves?

49. One model – one confusion matrix – one set of TPR/FPR pair. How do we get multiple TPR/FPR pairs to plot the ROC curve?

50. Why is TNR/FNR not considered in the ROC curve instead of TPR/FPR? How would the curve look when TNR/FNR is considered?

51. Explain gains table. What is the lift chart?

52. What is the KS statistic?

53. What is concordance/discordance?

54. What is the F score?

55. How do you train a model with imbalanced data (very low event rate)?

56. What kind of analytics can you do on a cricket match before it is played? After it is played? During the play?

57. What is the difference between Business Intelligence and Analytics?

58. What are the various node splitting criteria for building a decision tree?

59. Why is pruning necessary?

60. What do the terminal nodes signify in a classification decision tree?

61. What do the terminal nodes signify in a regression decision tree?

62. How can we stop the recursive splitting of nodes in a decision tree?

63. Explain one disadvantage of decision trees compared to linear regression.

64. What is the difference between a decision tree and a random forest?

65. What does the mtry parameter do in random forests using R?

66. What is the difference between K Means clustering and Hierarchical clustering?

67. What are the properties of a good clustering?

68. What are the diagnostics of K Means clustering?

69. What are the diagnostics of Hierarchical clustering?

70. What is WSS, BSS and strength of a clustering exercise?

71. In K Means clustering WSS should be high or low?

72. In K Means clustering BSS should be high or low?

73. How is the elbow curve useful in K Means clustering?

74. What do you understand by vanishing and exploding gradients?

75. How does backpropagation work?

76. What is the difference between neural networks and deep learning?

77. What are the disadvantages of using a sigmoid activation function in complex problems?

78. What is the primary purpose of a dropout layer?

79. What is the difference between RNN and CNN?

80. What is the difference between deep learning and machine learning?

81. What is the difference between text analytics and NLP?

82. Why do we have to remove stop words from the text before training a model?

83. What is a DTM? Can I merely build a model using the DTM?

84. Does text analytics use supervised or unsupervised learning?

85. What are multi-grams? TF/IDF? Cosine similarity?

86. What is bagging and boosting?

87. What is regularization?

88. What is cross-validation and how does it help?

89. How would you approach an analytics problem when the number of data points is very low (for example 100)?

90. What is an observation? What is a data point?

91. How would you carry out clustering with categorical variables?

92. What are support, confidence and lift in Association Mining?

93. What is Market Basket Analysis? What is the apriori algorithm?

94. Can you do cross-selling using MBA?

95. What is an item set?

96. Approximately how many rules are we talking about with 1000 transactions?

97. What are KNN, Naïve Bayes and SVM?

98. What is reinforcement learning?

99. What is Topic modeling? On what basis do the words associate itself to the topics?

100. What is Word2Vec? What are the 2 main underlying methods behind its functionality?

101. What are the implications of an imbalanced data set? What are the ways of handling data imbalance?

35. Analytics on This Book

Have the authors done a good job in naming the articles?

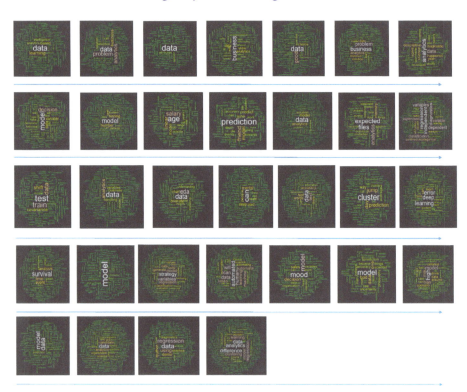

Word Cloud of Each Article in this Book

Word Clouds of Individual Articles in the Book

The word clouds tell us that the flow of focus in the book went as the following with each new article (not very strictly speaking). Note that we have deliberately skipped few word clouds from the flow of focus to let you experience that approximation and generalization are two excellent friends of a data scientist.

1. *Intelligence and learning of machines using data*

2. *Data related problems and solution adoption*

3. *Attributes of data and opinion*

4. *Business analytics*

5. *Choosing the right data scientists*

6. *Analytics solves business problems*

7. *Descriptive analytics and model diagnostics*

8. *Decisions using statistical models*

9. *Models helping in software testing*

10. *Linear relationship between age and salary*

11. *Prediction*

12. *Data Analytics*

13. *Expected files in production*

14. *Regression and independent variables*

15. *Test data and train data sets*

16. *Data analytics and business*

17. *Can (trust and ability)*

18. *Text*

19. *Cluster*

20. *Deep Learning*

21. *Survival, time and event*

22. *Analytics strategy*

23. *Automation*

24. *Mood as an attribute*

25. *Philosophy in analytics*

26. *Bias*

27. *Organization*

28. *Demo of an analytics solution*

29. *Difference between various analytics paired-terms*

Table Showing the Degree of Match

Serial Number	What Does Word Cloud Tell Us?	What Is the Actual Focus?	Degree of Match (High, Medium, Low)
1.	Intelligence and learning of machines using data	Understanding jargons	Medium
2.	Data related problems and solution adoption	Should analytics be the way to go?	Medium
3.	Attributes of data and opinion	Why should opinions be based on data?	High
4.	Business analytics	Uses of analytics	High
5.	Choosing the right data scientists	Attributes of a good data scientist	High
6.	Analytics solves business problems	A good data scientist builds solutions instead of models	Medium
7.	Descriptive analytics and model diagnostics	Discovering the past	Medium
8.	Decisions using statistical models	Historical data as a limitation of modeling	Low
9.	Models helping in software testing	Analytics for better test management	High
10.	Linear relationship between age and salary	Extrapolation of linearity	High
11.	Prediction	Predicting events	High
12.	Data Analytics	Various stages of an analytics project	Medium

Serial Number	What Does Word Cloud Tell Us?	What Is the Actual Focus?	Degree of Match (High, Medium, Low)
13.	Expected files in production	Documentation in analytics	Low
14.	Regression and independent variables	Summary of modeling techniques	Low
15.	Test data and train data sets	Test data should have a similar profile to train data	High
16.	Data analytics and business	Challenges in analytics	Low
17.	Can (trust and ability)	Importance of EDA	Low
18.	Text	Text analytics	High
19.	Cluster	Predict using clustering	High
20.	Deep Learning	Deep learning	High
21.	Survival, time and event	Survival analysis	High
22.	Analytics strategy	Customize models	Medium
23.	Automation	Automating machine learning	High
24.	Mood as an attribute	Machine replacing data scientist	Low
25.	Philosophy in analytics	Philosophy and analytics	High
26.	Bias	Bias-variance trade-off	High
27.	Organization	Where does data science fail?	Low
28.	Demo of an analytics solution	Interviews	Medium
29.	Difference between various analytics paired-terms	Questions	High

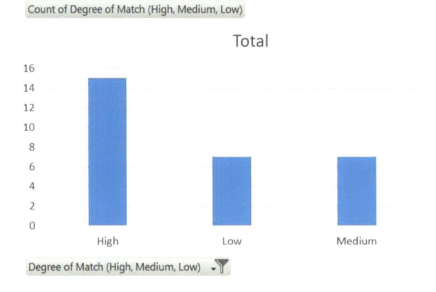

Bar Chart of Degree of Match

15 titles have a high match

7 titles have a medium match

7 titles have a low match

As seen in the above chart the word cloud suggestion

- Matches with the title given by the authors 51.7% of times

- Partially matches 24.1% of times

- Does not match 24.1% of times

We can say that the authors have done reasonably well in naming the articles.

What Is the Impact of Length of a Title in the Above Analysis?

Table Showing Title Lengths

Serial Number	Title of Article	Degree of Match (High, Medium, Low)	Length of Title (in characters)
1	Putting Jargon-olytics in Perspective	Medium	37
2	Analytics or Not. Checklist	Medium	27
3	Data Based Opinion Versus Opinion Based Opinion	High	47
4	Analytics. Where Do We Use?	High	27
5	What Makes A Good Data Scientist?	High	33
6	Don't Build a Model, Build a Solution	Medium	37
7	Predicting The Past	Medium	19
8	Predicting Better Than History	Low	30
9	Defect Prediction For Better Test Management	High	44
10	Predicting the Salary of a 120 Year Old!	High	40
11	Predicting Fortunate/Unfortunate Events	High	39
12	Hop a Little Jump a Little From Stage to Stage	Medium	46
13	Passing On To Next Generation	Low	29
14	Summarize Basic Modeling Techniques. Will You?	Low	46
15	Train and Test Datasets. Should they be Twins?	High	46
16	What Should the Data Science Practitioner Be Careful About?	Low	59
17	The Underplayed EDA	Low	19
18	Text Analytics in its Deceivingly Innocent Form	High	47
19	Predict Using Clustering. Really?	High	33
20	What is so deep about Deep Learning?	High	36
21	Survival Analysis	High	17
22	A Customized Ensemble Model	Medium	27
23	Machining Machine Learning	High	26
24	Can Machine Learning Replace its Master, the Data Scientist?	Low	60
25	When The Data Scientist in Me Becomes a Philosopher	High	51
26	Are You Too Generic or Too Specific? The Bias Variance Trade Off	High	64
27	When Can Data Science Fail?	Low	27
28	Data Science Interviews	Medium	23
29	No Negative Marks for Asking	High	28

High degree of match: average of 38.53 characters per title

Medium degree of match: average of 30.85 characters per title

Low degree of match: average of 38.57 characters per title

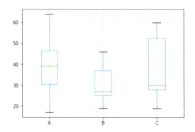

Box Plots of Degree of Match

X-axis: match categories

Y-axis: title lengths

A (high match)

B (medium match)

C (low match)

We see above a box plot of title lengths for each match category. A has a broader spread than C which in turn has a broader spread than B. Task for you. What insights can you find from the box plots? Can we say that shorter titles were better than longer titles?

What Is the Most Focused Entity in the Book?

Word Cloud of All Articles Taken Together

Data is the single most focused entity throughout the book for obvious reasons!

Emotion and Sentiment Analysis

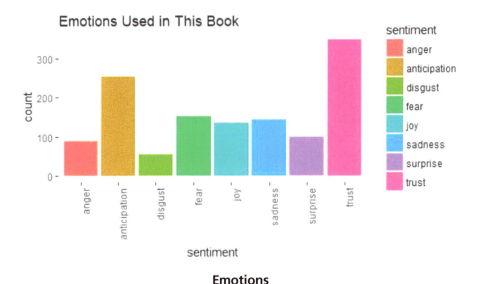

Emotions

Trust and anticipation are the winning emotions reflected in the book.

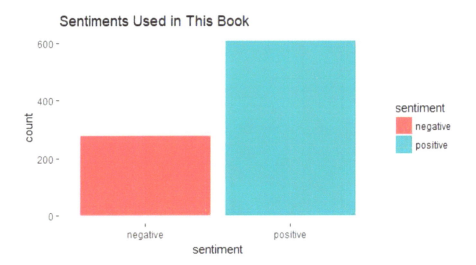

Sentiments

The authors have used more positive tones than negative tones.

Analysis on Words

Total number of words :   16751
Total number of sentences: 721

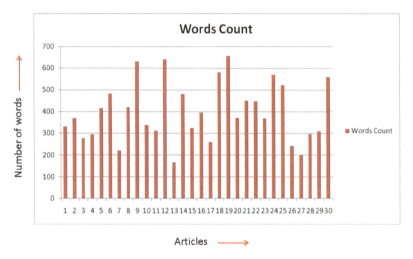

Word Count of Each Article

There are a total of 16751 words. Approximately 7% of the articles have less than 200 words and 90% of the articles have between 200 and 500 words indicating that authors have maintained uniformity and also covered sizeable information in each article.

Analysis on Sentences

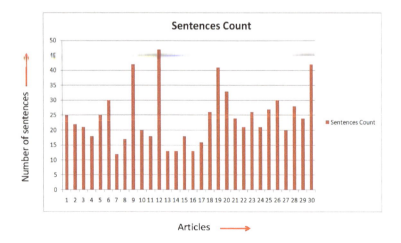

Sentence Count of Each Article

There are a total of 721 sentences. On average, there are about 15 sentences per article. 3 articles have sentences count of over 40 which can be treated as outliers. Last 10 articles show a smooth, gradual increase which means to suggest that forthcoming article will be more than 20 sentences on average.

Topic Modeling

```
Topic: 14
Words: ['data', 'model', 'analytics', 'using', 'one', 'variable', 'learning', 'problem']
Topic: 9
Words: ['data', 'model', 'analytics', 'variable', 'problem', 'could', 'using', 'test']
Topic: 11
Words: ['data', 'analytics', 'model', 'learning', 'business', 'one', 'problem', 'science']
Topic: 3
Words: ['data', 'model', 'business', 'problem', 'analytics', 'variable', 'learning', 'one']
Topic: 16
Words: ['data', 'model', 'analytics', 'using', 'problem', 'business', 'variable', 'one']
Topic: 10
Words: ['data', 'model', 'analytics', 'problem', 'business', 'one', 'using', 'science']
Topic: 2
Words: ['data', 'model', 'analytics', 'problem', 'test', 'one', 'science', 'variable']
Topic: 8
Words: ['data', 'model', 'analytics', 'using', 'learning', 'science', 'machine', 'problem']
Topic: 18
Words: ['data', 'model', 'analytics', 'one', 'variable', 'science', 'could', 'problem']
Topic: 0
Words: ['data', 'model', 'analytics', 'variable', 'problem', 'using', 'one', 'test']
```

Topic Modeling

Topic modeling applied to the entire contents of this book. This is unsupervised learning where each topic is assigned with a set of frequently occurring words corresponding to the topic number. Data, model and analytics are the top words in almost all topics with 80% coverage.

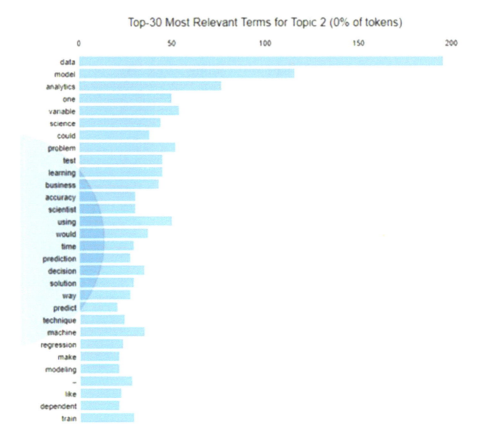

Relevant Terms for Topic 2

Graphical representation of topic modeling output created on Jupyter notebook where the controls are interactive and the graphs update automatically.

N-gram representations

Six-grams with most frequent terms appearing together

```
[(('and', 'test', 'the', 'following', 'models', 'for'), 3),
 (('the', 'Salary', 'of', 'a', '120', 'Year'), 2),
 (('a', 'Little', 'Jump', 'a', 'Little', 'From'), 2),
 (('Little', 'Jump', 'a', 'Little', 'From', 'Stage'), 2),
 (('Jump', 'a', 'Little', 'From', 'Stage', 'to'), 2),
 (('and', 'Test', 'Datasets.', 'Should', 'they', 'be'), 2),
 (('Should', 'the', 'Data', 'Science', 'Practitioner', 'Be'), 2),
 (('the', 'Data', 'Science', 'Practitioner', 'Be', 'Careful'), 2),
 (('Machine', 'Learning', 'Replace', 'its', 'Master', 'the'), 2),
 (('Learning', 'Replace', 'its', 'Master,', 'the', 'Data'), 2)]
```

Quad-grams with most frequent terms appearing together

```
[(('is', 'the', 'difference', 'between'), 14),
 (('in', 'the', 'form', 'of'), 5),
 (('are', 'the', 'diagnostics', 'of'), 5),
 (('be', 'a', 'good', 'data'), 4),
 (('of', 'System', 'testing', 'defects'), 4),
 (('can', 'be', 'used', 'in'), 4),
 (('can', 'also', 'be', 'used'), 4),
 (('the', 'train', 'and', 'test'), 3),
 (('number', 'of', 'System', 'testing'), 3),
 (('I', 'am', 'going', 'to'), 3)]
```

Bi grams with most frequent terms

```
[(('of', 'the'), 55),
 (('in', 'the'), 45),
 (('is', 'the'), 34),
 (('the', 'model'), 30),
 (('of', 'a'), 29),
 (('is', 'a'), 28),
 (('can', 'be'), 23),
 (('could', 'be'), 22),
 (('are', 'the'), 22),
 (('on', 'the'), 22)]
```

n-grams

N-gram representations show which words frequently occur when placed together. N represents the number of words occurring together. Here you can see that more than bi-grams, we can make sense of 6-gram where we can get to know for example when Machine word is present there is an instance of Learning also appearing along with other words with high frequencies.

Predicting the Content of Our Next Book

Predicting Future Articles

Our Book

Next article written by machine

This model was trained on entire contents of the book which has over 89770 characters and over 10000 patterns.

Prediction Output

" ndidate come across as in that one hour? don't forget to focus on the importance of how the organization came across through the interviewer in that one hour. every word the interviewer speaks is, in effect, on behalf of the organization.
honesty
hon "

Predicting Future Articles

Did you go through the output? Does it make sense? It may not. That is because the historical data used for training the model was very less. With a good volume of training data and model tuning, this can be used to generate the next article automatically or might even be our next book on analytics!

We hope that you found this book enjoyable and informative.

Sample Feedback from Readers

1. This is a great guide because it captures the strong essence of Data Science and its approaches without diluting the topics. This is uncommon in most of the handouts, at least in my experience so far. I think the authors made it very interesting with the examples and the analogies picked to explain a subject in a simple way. Moreover, the icing on the cake is the titles and their captions. Thoroughly enjoyed them. For a Data Science aspirant like me, this is a perfect reference book. Of course, the highlight of all is the text analytics performed on the content of the book itself. The output of the sentiment analysis very evidently brings out the positivity of the book.

   Partha Vijayan, Budding data scientist, Verizon India, Chennai.

2. A delightful guide which is full of important information for those who are data science enthusiasts. This is a great book and a must read primer to start with.

   Neelakanta Matadam, Data Science enthusiast, Verizon India, Hyderabad.

3. Data became my new obsession. Reading the book was like looking at the analytics world through a magnifying glass.

   Sriram Lamsal, M.Tech. student and placement coordinator and data science aspirant, College of Engineering and Technology, Bhubaneswar.

4. The authors take your thoughts to a different side of data analytics. It is a must-read book for anyone looking to embark on a lifelong journey towards enlightenment through analytics.

   M. Yogananth, AVP, HSBC, Chennai.

5. The authors have poured their distilled expertise in data science into this book. This is a must-have book for all the analytics professionals. This is different from what a purely technical book or a purely statistical book would have offered. The authors have given very useful and practical insights.

   Radhakrishnan Guhan, Data Scientist, TCS, Chennai.

6. "The book is good, simple and easy to understand."

   Vrushali Sarfare, Consultant in a large IT organization, Mumbai.